MW01060578

Praise for Pipe Dreams

"With her trademark meticulous reporting, Erin Banco brings us the woefully untold story of theft in Iraq: the robbing of the Iraqi people's natural resource rights. She takes us behind the scenes of broken promises and charts an ongoing network of corruption and deceit that continued to plunder not only Iraq's oil wealth, but also its would-be beneficiaries. The result is a journalistic tour de force that can't be ignored."

—**Lauren Bohn,**
Co-founder of Foreign Policy Interrupted and
Middle East correspondent for The GroundTruth Project

"Erin Banco expertly tells the complicated story of corruption that lies at the heart of the endless problems gripping Kurdistan and greater Iraq. Her investigative work on the country's troubled oil industry is deeply researched and engagingly told—and it shows how mismanagement and greed have turned a resource that should be a blessing into a curse. The book offers a unique and timely window onto the country's tumultuous past, as well as a lens for understanding the instability and violence that continue to plague it today."

—**Mike Giglio,**
Buzzfeed

Pipe Dreams
The Plundering of
Iraq's Oil Wealth

COLUMBIA GLOBAL REPORTS
NEW YORK

Pipe Dreams
The Plundering of Iraq's Oil Wealth

Erin Banco

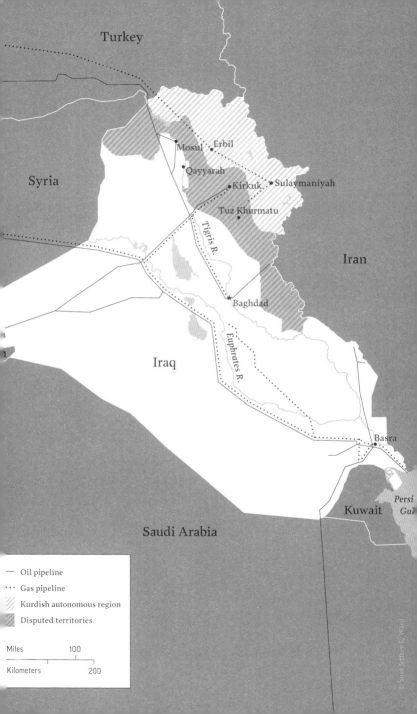

Turkey

Syria

Mosul
Erbil
Qayyarah
Kirkuk
Sulaymaniyah
Tuz Khurmatu

Tigris R.

Iran

Baghdad

Euphrates R.

Iraq

Basra

Saudi Arabia

Kuwait

Persi
Gul

— Oil pipeline
••• Gas pipeline
//// Kurdish autonomous region
//// Disputed territories

Miles   100
Kilometers   200

Pipe Dreams
The Plundering of Iraq's Oil Wealth

Copyright © 2018 by Erin Banco
All rights reserved

Published by Columbia Global Reports
91 Claremont Avenue, Suite 515
New York, NY 10027
globalreports.columbia.edu
facebook.com/columbiaglobalreports
@columbiaGR

Library of Congress Control Number: 2016962880
ISBN: 978-0997722949

Book design by Strick&Williams
Map design by Jeffrey L. Ward
Author photograph by Miranda Sita

Printed in the United States of America

For Mom and Dad
With love and gratitude

CONTENTS

Return of the Resource Curse

Fouad Hussein's Lexus SUV roared down the dusty highway on the outskirts of Kirkuk. Hussein, so optimistic just a few years back, was taking me on a dispiriting tour as he unwound a dispiriting story. It was the winter of 2016, and Iraq was in its third year of war against ISIS. Just over fifty miles south, in the town of Tuz Khurmatu, Kurdish militias were facing off against Shiite fighters backed by the Iraqi central government, both vying for greater control over Kirkuk. The war, Hussein said, was not just about defeating a terrorist organization, but about political factions and armies fighting for control and influence.

As Hussein and I drove, we passed by refugee camps. The battle with ISIS had sucked the region dry of cash and contributed to one of the worst humanitarian disasters in recent history. As bad, some international oil companies had begun to wonder whether Iraqi Kurdistan was the investment opportunity it was advertised to be following the U.S. invasion. Fed up with disappointing exploration results coupled with years of instability and a frustrating oil ministry, some oil companies had pulled out of the region. Several oil companies were in debt and had not received payouts from the cash-strapped Kurdistan Regional Government as promised in their contracts. Civil servants, despite raucous demands, had not been paid by the government in months.

Hussein, a member of the province's oil and gas committee, was elected to the council in 2005. Hussein has lived in Kirkuk most of his life, decades in which the city has been fought over constantly. He saw it subjected to the Anfal campaign of genocide under former President Saddam Hussein, who sought to contain Kurdish aspirations for self-determination. He saw his friends die fighting for Kurdish rights and freedom and witnessed Kurdish homes completely leveled by Saddam's military. And then, upon the ousting of Saddam, he saw hundreds of thousands of people begin to hope.

Foreign energy companies slowly arrived in the late 1990s, and then en masse following the American invasion in 2003, with plans to develop Iraqi Kurdistan into one of the most productive oil and natural gas regions in the Middle East. Despite the Kurds' lingering tensions with the Baghdad government, a new, wildly prosperous era seemed just over the horizon. More than ten years later, Hussein said, those dreams were in tatters. Initial hopes that things would turn out for the better have mostly resulted in disappointment.

The fight between Kurdish and Iraqi militias dramatically escalated in late 2017, following a Kurdish referendum for

14   independence. After the vote, Iraqi forces moved into Kirkuk, taking over key positions the Kurds had guarded since 2014, and control of the oilfields changed hands. The intense stand-off not only escalated tensions between Baghdad and Erbil, but also caused internal rifts between the Kurdish main political parties and their soldiers. The skirmishes seemed to wipe away any hope by the Kurds that they would soon solidify their control in Kirkuk and gain full autonomy from the central government.

The extreme swings of war and terrorism, going back to the early days of Saddam and even before, have left their mark on the Iraqi people. Millions of ordinary Iraqis have been displaced from their homes. Thousands of people, both Iraqi and American, have died. That story, chronically recycled by news outlets, certainly deserves to be told. But a more complicated story—and yet no less important one—is the promise made to the Iraqis that after the bombs and bullets stopped flying, after Saddam had been vanquished, their lives would be made immeasurably better. One of the reasons? Because Iraq and Iraqi Kurdistan sit on some of the world's largest oil reserves. And in times of peace, billions of dollars could flow from those oil riches into the public coffers, replacing chaos and poverty with prosperity and plenty.

It hasn't worked out that way for Iraqi Kurdistan.

This book tells the story of the government's actions in Iraqi Kurdistan, how squabbling, coupled with the introduction of Western oil companies in the region, robbed the Iraqi people of their natural resource rights. The story is complex:

Pipe Dreams is not all-encompassing. It tells just a sliver of the   15
larger narrative of oil corruption in Iraqi Kurdistan. This book
is not about the technicalities of Iraqi Kurdistan's oil industry,
or the nuances of production and sales, though it does touch
on some of these subjects. It instead focuses on what happened
behind the scenes between the Kurdish government and international oil companies—negotiations, payouts, and kickbacks
that exacerbated the plundering of the region's oil. It explores
the effort by corporations to take advantage of a crumbling
country engulfed in war, and a regional government's vision of
gaining greater autonomy from Baghdad through oil sales. All of
this unfolds in the context of a political climate rife with financial rivalries, constant war, and an economic crisis triggered in
part by teetering oil prices and an influx of refugees.

It should be noted that this story—the resource curse in
Iraqi Kurdistan—is one shared with the people who live elsewhere in Iraq, under the leadership of the central government
in Baghdad. Oil corruption exists there, too, but the story in
Baghdad looks different, because the Iraqi government uses a
completely different model to govern its oil sector. As you read
this book, know that much of what unfolded in Iraqi Kurdistan
is a product, at least in part, of the political and military position in Baghdad and its relationship to the West, most notably
the U.S.

In more than a hundred interviews conducted for this
book, the people in Iraqi Kurdistan told me they thought
their lives would improve once oil giants set up shop. They
said they expected more job opportunities. Some thought the

16   mere presence of wealthy companies would bring prosperity. Although many of them worry about their safety and the war against ISIS, they also worry about how they are going to put food on the table at night. It is a worry propelled and exacerbated in part by the government's corruption and by the failed promises that first came from politicians and oil companies during the U.S. invasion to overthrow Saddam.

The money from oil did flow, but little of it has reached ordinary Kurdish people, either directly or in the form of regional projects. While oil revenues have funded the Kurdish military in its fight against ISIS, big sums have been siphoned off in a web of corruption, whereby some in the Kurdish political elite created a system of pay-to-play contracts and kickbacks that enriched themselves while the people of Iraqi Kurdistan lived through a financial crisis. By some accounts, billions of dollars have disappeared to fraud.

Indeed, Iraqi Kurdistan seems a classic example of the resource curse. Oil is found, pumped, shipped, and sold (and sometimes stolen). Regimes, politicians, ministers, and companies come and go. And yet the average person benefits marginally or not all. If the generic chaos of war, terrorism, and political infighting explains some of this, it doesn't explain it all. For the Kurds, greed and fraud, tolerated if not abetted by U.S. and multinational oil companies, also lie at the center of their dashed oil dreams.

The corruption starts within Kurdistan's ministries, particularly in the Ministry of Natural Resources, and is fueled by rivalries in the political system. Interviews with financial enforcement officers in the U.S. and the UK, and a study of the thousands of pages of documents they gave me, reveal the ministry and its political allies in the Kurdish leadership often sold off valuable oil assets to shell companies in the British Virgin Islands and other tax havens. Then, it quickly flipped the assets for huge profits to major international oil companies listed on stock exchanges in London, Canada, Oslo, and New York. In other scenarios, subsidiaries of shell corporations paid the Kurdish government for oil blocks. The government then transferred some of that money to accounts earmarked for companies whose hidden owners were members of the main political parties.

Some major American players in this scenario have defended U.S. corporate involvement, noting that post-Saddam, the Iraqis and Kurds themselves were eager to develop their oil resources and in some cases all but begged Americans to enter into exploration and production-sharing contracts. But ordinary Kurds have grown cynical of this benevolent explanation, particularly when they see how some former high-ranking Bush administration officials who had advocated for the overthrow of Saddam leveraged their government positions, contacts, and insider knowledge to make huge fortunes from Iraqi and Kurdistan oil investments. Today, some of those very people continue to sit on the boards of, or have lucrative jobs as advisors to, those very same multinational oil firms.

The U.S. State Department, in documents released by WikiLeaks, was aware that corruption was a way of life in Kurdistan, where elite Kurdish families with deep tribal and political connections were complicit in creating the web by which they've

18   enriched themselves. Part of the difficulty is that in a place with little transparency, where corruption has long been a fact of life and where journalism is often just a front for political parties to embarrass rivals, truth, impartial reporting, and honest data are hard to come by. Meanwhile, Iraq and the Kurdistan region are dangerous places for journalists to work, with as many as 145 attacks against journalists just in the year 2015.

During my time reporting as Middle East Correspondent for *International Business Times*, and then afterward as a freelance journalist, I covered the rise of ISIS in Iraq. Part of that coverage included reporting on the group's economic network and its sale of stolen oil. It was in that time I often spoke to oil workers on the ground, consultants working for oil companies, and Washington analysts. I cultivated a source who had worked in the Kurdish oil game and knew the players well. The source worked in Washington as an expert: We talked often about ISIS and how the war impacted the Iraqi economy. Eventually, our conversations turned almost exclusively into discussions about oil and the Western firms that work in the Kurdistan Regional Government. In the summer of 2014, many of the companies were on alert—unsure about pulling their people out of the country and whether the war would hurt sales. The source eventually introduced me to people who worked in the financial regulatory fields. I spent years talking with them.

They started sending me documents, usually one at a time, but sometimes batches at once. It seemed that they wanted to expose the details of cases that either never went anywhere, that were kept under wraps for political reasons, or that were

still under investigation but had not moved forward. I created
binders and filed each of them away, studying their contents at
night. All of the documents went through several levels of fact
checks.

This book relies in part on testimony from former U.S.
and UK regulatory enforcement officers who worked for years
investigating corruption in Iraq's natural resource sector. I've
received hundreds of documents detailing transactions between
the Ministry of Natural Resources and multinational oil companies that these investigators say are thinly disguised kickbacks
that are part of a web of corrupt conduct.

This system has developed cracks, in part because U.S. and
other multinational oil companies, all too happy to jump into
Kurdistan when they realized billions could be made, have been
less happy recently. For some, the very ministry that induced
them to come to Iraqi Kurdistan began rewriting their lucrative
contracts. Then, as ISIS squeezed off oil production and the refugee crisis peaked, the ministry failed to pay billions of dollars
in payments the companies say they were owed. Several of these
disputes have played out in courts in London. These cases shed
light on the inner workings of the Ministry of Natural Resources
and how and why it created its chaotic, corruption-prone oil contracts system.

Oil revenue numbers in Iraq are difficult to decipher. Many
of the reports do not separate Baghdad's revenue from Kurdistan's. Other specific oil data is held only by industry analysts
and is not always available to the public. But by one estimate, oil
in Iraq has produced more than $700 billion in revenues since

20   2003—indeed, oil income accounts for about 80 percent of all of Iraq's funding. Yet Baghdad and Kurdistan today are failing to pay public salaries. Oil analysts have said years of mismanagement caused the government to misuse its oil revenues in a way that leaves little money for things like schools and infrastructure.

Estimates of the losses to fraud and mismanagement in Iraq as a whole are staggering—or perhaps not surprising for a country ranked sixth from the bottom (out of 167 nations) on Transparency International's 2015 Corruption Perceptions Index. Corruption and mismanagement could have cost Iraq and Iraqi Kurdistan $20 billion just in the year 2013, according to a report by an analyst at Columbia University. The British Serious Fraud Office is said to be looking into allegations that Monaco-based Unaoil has been involved in widespread corruption, channeling huge bribes to Baghdad government officials in exchange for helping Unaoil clients (including some British firms such as Rolls-Royce) to win billions of dollars in contracts. Unaoil has denied the allegations and in a statement said it had ordered its lawyers to "commence legal proceedings" against various news organizations. In 2016, the Iraqi Parliament's Integrity Commission finally began looking into the alleged Unaoil bribes, but so far no one in Iraq or the Kurdistan region has been criminally prosecuted for oil-sector corruption.

On the ground in Kurdistan, people are hurting as the economy is in a tailspin: A mother I interviewed in a house on the outskirts of Kirkuk can't pay for a doctor to cure her son's skin rash; a twelve-year-old boy who each day sits on a bucket on the side of the highway in Erbil begging construction trucks to stop and hire him. These people remain cynical about not just their political process, but ours, too.

Many Iraqis said they thought Western interventionism still felt as potent as ever. They said they felt their country had never truly been given back to them. Most were not optimistic that it would change anytime soon, despite the passing of a referendum for Kurdish autonomy in the fall of 2017. The fight against ISIS continues, and meanwhile, there is today a new leader in the White House who seems to know little about Iraq and even less about its oil politics, despite having former ExxonMobil CEO Rex Tillerson as Secretary of State, a man who in many ways dominated the oil sector in the Kurdistan region for years.

On the day after he was sworn in as the forty-fifth president in American history, Donald Trump gave a speech at the CIA, saying that although he didn't approve of the Iraqi invasion, he thought the U.S. should have done more to profit off of the country's natural resources. "We should have kept the oil," he said.

In a way, we did.

Capital of the Oil Mirage

Kirkuk, seen through the sand-matted windows of our car, is bustling with energy, but some of the city's walls are cracking. As we enter the sprawling oil town from the highway on a stultifying day in August 2016, two things are apparent: the suffocating heat and a crumbling city center.

Al-Qaeda in Iraq and ISIS have waged war near here over the years, and it shows. Drab tan concrete structures with cracked windows and collapsing roofs dominate the architecture. Blast barricades, put up by the Americans during the invasion of 2003, surround many downtown government buildings. Happy murals of fields and Kurdish men dancing on mountaintops decorate these imposing barriers, giving them a surreal quality.

The war against ISIS is headed into another tense month, and cells of the terrorist group continue to operate here. Still, students are going to school, men still occupy their fruit stands, women and children occupy local playgrounds. Our car passes by one of the oldest parts of the city—the ancient citadel, located on a plateau that extends across the Khasa River. A teal dome-shaped figure sits atop the plateau. In its shadow stands a busy open market that spans a bridge over the river. Vendors hawk clothing, food, home products, and all manner of things you might find in a U.S. hardware store. Piles of trash—soda cans, cardboard boxes, and plastic bags—line the riverbank beneath the bridge.

Kirkuk, with a population of 850,000 and rising (and 1.26 million throughout the wider governorate), sits surrounded by a vast expanse of dust and rock, of seemingly unending, feature-less desert where sporadic islands of grass wage a losing battle to hang on in the relentless heat. On the drive in, all that breaks the monotony of the horizon are clusters of oil wells in the dis-tance and brown rounded hills beyond. But as Fouad Hussein will inform me on my several visits to see him, this bleak land-scape sits atop beautiful mountains of oil coveted not just by the Kurds and other Iraqis but also by the West and its oil com-panies—indeed, by the world.

The bustling city center can't mask the fact that tensions are high here and throughout Iraqi Kurdistan. The all-out as-sault to push ISIS from its last strongholds—most importantly, Mosul, a hundred miles to the northwest, and the oil-rich city of Qayyarah—may yet be several months away, but prepa-rations are already in full swing. The Kurdish military—the Peshmerga—has been holding joint exercises with U.S. mili-tary advisors and Iraqi army regulars from Baghdad. The rattle, groan, and thrum of military vehicles has become the back-ground noise here.

Meanwhile, Kirkuk security forces are busy tracking down and infiltrating ISIS cells. ISIS is not just setting off death-dealing car bombs; it is actively recruiting and training men to use the city as a launching base for attacks. Just a month after I finished my Kirkuk reporting, ISIS members launched a massive attack on the Kurdish troops stationed here, killing security officers and taking several hostages in a local hotel before being killed themselves.

Making this situation even more precarious, Kirkuk finds itself in August 2016 in a dispute with both the Kurdish government in Erbil and the central government in Baghdad. When ISIS rose to power in June of 2014, the Baghdad-controlled Iraqi military abandoned many of its Kurdistan posts, including ones in Kirkuk. The Kurdish military moved in and took over those bases. That move exacerbated a forty-year-long political battle between the two governments and an even longer dispute between different ethnic groups.

In fact, nothing about Kirkuk seems settled. Iraq is a federation, which means the country is composed of several different states that each have some degree of autonomy. Kurdistan is a federal state within Iraq and includes three governorates: Duhok, Erbil, and Sulaymaniyah. Within those governorates lie three different provinces with their own local governments. Kirkuk consists of Arabs, Kurds, and Turkmen, and Assyrian Christians, Sunnis, and Shiites. Several of Iraq's ethnic groups consider Kirkuk their ancestral homeland, and view themselves as the city's rightful rulers. They have fought endlessly over control of the city and the greater governorate. One scholar

likens the Kurdish affiliation with Kirkuk to the Jewish and Arab
affiliation with Jerusalem.

The ISIS invasion and the subsequent abandonment by the Iraqi military of Kurdistan outposts saw the Kurds usurp oil operations previously overseen by Baghdad's state-run North Oil Company. And the governorate is in flux, overseen by a local council made up of Arabs, Kurds, and Turkmen that ostensibly operates above the political fray but in fact is riven by all the fractures and rivalries that animate the larger political battle. Although each provincial council member claims to work on behalf of the larger population in Kirkuk, many of them answer to their party heads, who actively oppose one another. Even Kurdish military forces, backed by either the PUK (Patriotic Union of Kurdistan) or the rival KDP (Kurdish Democratic Party), are at odds: Ever since the rise of ISIS they have vied for control over Kirkuk's oil.

To get a flavor of how things are going on the ground, I catch up with Fouad Hussein. Hussein's city center office is located in a building that was formerly used by American and British forces during the 2003 Iraq War. Now, it has almost no security. A rickety metal gate opens on to a main courtyard. The complex looks abandoned. Many of the windows don't have screens or glass.

Men dressed in military uniforms lead us up a set of concrete stairs, past a flooded bathroom, into a room filled with couches. This is where Hussein holds local government meetings. White lace curtains hang over cracked windows. Hussein's cluttered, dusty desk anchors one end of the room. Behind it

26   stands a gold pole with the red, white, and green Kurdistan flag, with its signature bright yellow sun in the center.

I've arrived in the broiling August heat, in the midst of a crisis that seems to be coming to an end but not without a fury of phone calls and negotiations. Hussein, a pair of reading glasses perched on the end of his nose, shuffles through a stack of papers as he frantically fields calls from other local officials. They are attempting to sort out a simmering dispute with the Baghdad government over oil export. After years of discord on this particular dispute, both sides are close to coming to an understanding. A member of the provincial council, wearing a tie and wrinkled overcoat despite the heat, sits nearby.

Hussein lays out the quandary: Baghdad has stopped sending money to the Kurds as retribution for them selling oil independently on the international market. In late 2014, the Kurdish government struck a deal that gave Iraq's central government access to revenue from Kurdish oil, in exchange for Baghdad paying the Kurds a sum equal to 17 percent of the federal budget. Kurdish oil, which accounts for about 15 percent of the crude Iraq currently produces, would be sold through Iraq's state-owned Oil Marketing Company, known as SOMO.

The rub, according to Hussein, was that while the Kurds were keeping their part of the deal, Baghdad had reneged on its promised 17-percent payments. As a result, the Kurds had no choice but to cut SOMO production and ramp up their own independent oil sales distributed through Turkey. But those sales had not been able to make up for the shortfall. The result was an earthquake

in the Kurdish economy. The drastic drop in exports forced the
Kurdish Ministry of Natural Resources to default on payments to
international oil companies operating in the region.

Baghdad had its own side of the story. Officials there claimed
it was the Kurds who were reneging. "Baghdad didn't pay what
Kurdistan was asking for because Kurdistan didn't give Baghdad
what it was supposed to," Jabbar Abdul Khaliq, an Iraqi lawmaker,
told *The Wall Street Journal* in July 2015. Baghdad claimed that the
oil from Kirkuk never went through SOMO, but was rather sold
to international trading houses that the Kurdish government had
set up contracts with dating back to 2013.

The original deal had strict stipulations, stating that the
Kurdistan Regional Government would deliver 550,000 barrels
of oil per day, including 300,000 from Kirkuk, but some reports
show that the KRG did not produce close to that number. Tariq
Gardi, a member of the Oil and Energy Committee in Iraq's Parliament, told *Al-Monitor* that the Kurds had failed to honor
the agreement. "This is a partial fulfillment of the deal, a new
approach taken by the KRG," Gardi said. When the KRG did
finally reach 550,000 barrels in April 2015, it claimed it still did
not receive payment from Baghdad.

"The Iraqi government hasn't handled this well," Hussein tells me, eyeing a nearby television. Scenes of burning oil
wells—sabotaged by ISIS months before and still on fire—
stream across the screen. "This oil is now being stored in refineries waiting to be transported," he says. "Some of it is being
bottled up and sold on the black market" by Kurdish smugglers.

28   Hussein is a member of the Kurdish Democratic Party in the local Kirkuk government. The KDP governs the larger Iraqi Kurdistan region, along with its erstwhile rival and co-ruler, the Patriotic Union of Kurdistan, headed by the first Kurdish President of Iraq, Jalal Talabani, who died in October 2017. Hussein joined the KDP after spending years as a refugee in Iran. In 1976, the KDP was looking for a fresh generation of leaders after the split that saw the founding of the PUK following the KDP's defeat in 1975. Hussein worked as a community organizer here, helping families with social issues before attending the government's oil and gas institute. He became a member of Kirkuk's provincial council oil and gas committee in 2005, which places him squarely in the middle of trying to sort out the latest dispute with Baghdad—not an easy job in this period of chronic instability. Endless citizen complaints keep him up at night. So do the occasional death threats from what he says are people affiliated with the opposition party.

"I am a community person," Hussein tells me. "I like to be with the people. I'm from Kirkuk. I understand people's problems. I am trying my best to serve their oil and gas needs. I receive letters from people every day complaining about things."

One issue is that Kirkuk's administration hasn't held elections since 2005, when the provincial council formed. Attempts since then have been blocked by the Independent High Electoral Commission of Iraq. The governorate was, however, able to vote for deputies to the national parliament in 2010 and 2014. "The constitution gives us the right to hold elections, but the central

government has blocked us from holding them," Hussein says.
"We need to get back this freedom. . . . The people of Kirkuk
have had their rights stripped away by Baghdad. There are no
jobs for them, no infrastructure."

After the American invasion of 2003, the Iraqi Parliament
couldn't come to an agreement on how to hold elections in
Kirkuk because it was unclear who was eligible to vote. Arabs
and Turkmen said the Kurdistan Regional Government had
moved Kurds to Kirkuk to create a majority that would help
them win a referendum that would incorporate the region into
Iraqi Kurdistan. The Kurdish government disputed that claim,
and said the Kurds had been forcibly removed under Saddam's
Arabization policy and were the rightful owners of the land.
By the end of 2005, more than 20,000 families who had been
forced out of Kirkuk did move back, according to the International Organization for Migration.

The Americans allowed Kurdish military and police forces to
maintain order after the invasion, which alarmed many minorities in the region, who thought it was simply an excuse to crack
down on the opposition. Arabs and Turkmens said they were
marginalized and resigned from the Kurdish provincial council
in protest; they only agreed to rejoin after a power-sharing deal in
2008. Under that deal, the provincial governor is supposed to be
a Kurd, while his two deputies must be an Arab and a Turkmen.
Regional elections were supposed to take place in November
2017, but they have been pushed back because of disputes with
Baghdad and the ongoing war against ISIS.

30   Hussein tells me that these matters have had a huge economic impact on his city, because they have wreaked havoc on the oil trade, even as the Kurds' reliance on the business has intensified. I had interviewed Hussein on another trip to Iraqi Kurdistan in 2015, around the time the Kurds had begun pumping their disputed oil to the international market via Turkey. Those were more hopeful days. The battle over Kirkuk is a metaphor for the greater fight between the Kurdish government in Erbil and the central government in Baghdad. The Kurds want independence from Baghdad, and oil is their only way out.

The story of that struggle begins in the early hours of October 15, 1927, when oil workers from the Turkish Petroleum Company were walking on the sandy fields of Kirkuk, which was then part of the British Empire. Months of wildcatting had produced no results—until that morning, when a well struck a payload so enormous that oil shot more than 130 meters into the air. This was the Baba Gurgur oil field, the largest in the world for more than two decades, until oil was discovered in the Ghawar field in Saudi Arabia in 1948.

The find of Baba Gurgur kickstarted the establishment of the oil sector in Iraq—and with it, economic growth that offered far more potential than the existing herder-agrarian-based economy. Development came in fits and starts, taking more than seven decades. It took twenty years after the discovery of Baba Gurgur before experienced international energy firms began their exploration operations in the country. But then, everyone wanted a piece of the Iraqi oil action.

World oil production skyrocketed in the 1950s after World
War II. The industry had previously been dominated by just a
few companies, but with the massive expansion of oil exploration and low barriers to entry, hundreds of other private and
state-owned firms entered the market. The Organization of
Petroleum Exporting Countries in 1960 started a new wave of
nationalism in the oil sector, with orthodox new thinking that
countries should maintain total control over energy resources.
For Iraq, nationalization of the oil sector came in the 1970s with
the rise of the Ba'athist regime, a political party that fostered
pan-Arabism. What began as a socialist party and helped build
Iraq's economy at first, metamorphosed into a dictatorship
under Saddam Hussein.

The United Kingdom had carved out the modern state
of Iraq after World War I. The Kurds, an ethnic minority in
modern-day Iraq, Turkey, Iran, and Syria, were promised independence in the Treaty of Sevres in 1920, but it was never
implemented. Its successor, the Treaty of Lausanne in 1923,
established the new Republic of Turkey—but didn't mention
the Kurds. Kurdish intellectuals and nationalists began to orga-
nize politically on various fronts in pursuit of conflicting goals.
The Kurds in Turkey organized resistance in the face of massacres and forced migration in the 1930s, including to Syria.
The Soviet Union initially supported Kurdish nationalism
when they invaded Iran in 1941, where a strip of the country's
northwest was declared the independent Kurdish Republic of
Mahabad in 1946. But months later the Soviets were pressured

32   by Western powers to withdraw their forces, and by the end of
the year the Iranian army took Mahabad, executing its leaders.
The republic's defense minister and military commander, Mustafa Barzani, fled to the Soviet Union and eventually returned
to Iraq, where he established the Kurdistan Democratic Party.
Barzani led the Kurdish rebellion against Iraq in 1961, and the
agreement that came out of the uprising established the Kurdish
Autonomous Region in 1970. In 1975, Jalal Talabani broke with
Barzani and formed the Patriotic Union of Kurdistan. The KDP
and the PUK have vied for control of Iraqi Kurdistan to this day.

When Saddam Hussein came to power, he initially tried to
negotiate with the PUK, but those efforts fell through in 1985. In
the last few years of the Iran-Iraq War, Saddam's Anfal genocide
killed more than 100,000 Kurds through destructions of entire
villages, mass executions, concentration camps, chemical
attacks, and military operations. The campaign's "Arabization"
also drove many Kurds from their homes, particularly in Kirkuk
(which itself holds about 10 percent of Iraq's oil reserves), and
forced them to the south.

Saddam seized control of the oil wealth of northern Iraq
from the Kurds, but his failed invasion of Kuwait eventually
returned it to them: The international coalition created a safe
haven and a no-fly zone in Iraqi Kurdistan and another in the
Shiite majority area in the south of the country, keeping Hussein's ambitions in check, and the Kurds began to acquire
greater autonomy from Baghdad. But rivalry between the KDP
and PUK erupted into an all-out civil conflict in the 1990s,
though the two parties were somehow able to maintain their

good relations with the West all along, which gave them an advantage during the second U.S. invasion of Iraq, in 2003. The border of Iraqi Kurdistan was expanded to the south during the invasion, and the Kurdish leadership gained access to more resources, including water and oil. Peshmerga fighters provided ground support to U.S. forces, while also directly seizing control of Kirkuk from the Iraqi Army.

That changed abruptly in September of 2017, when the Kurdish people voted for independence from Iraq in a referendum backed by the KDP but initially opposed by the PUK. The move infuriated central governments in Baghdad, Iran, and Turkey, which all immediately declared it invalid. By October, Iraqi forces pushed the Kurds out of their positions in Kirkuk, seizing the surrounding oilfields, pushing the ongoing tensions between Erbil and Baghdad to an all-time high.

"Let's take a drive," Hussein tells me. He steers his white Lexus on a northward path from the city to show me evidence of the unfolding disaster. He's an energetic man for someone who sleeps just a few hours a night and spends his days trying to figure out how to bring more money into his community. In crisp khakis and a blue buttoned up, long-sleeve cotton shirt, he slows the car, flicking a wilting cigarette from the window, and points to columns of black smoke and oil dust clouds in the distance.

"This is the biggest area for oil in the country, but for some reason we can't seem to get it right," he says, shaking his head. The fires have been flaring for days in and around Kirkuk. Oil

34   exports through the main pipeline to Turkey have stopped, cutting the amount of Kurdish crude being shipped from 512,000 barrels per day to 430,000 in just one month. According to Alan Mohtadi, an oil consultant working with companies in the KRG, the 2017 oil production before the referendum was up to about 620,000 barrels a day.

Hussein pulls over and hops out of the car. He clambers up a jumbled dirt mound that acts as a de facto barrier between the road and a parallel ditch. "The most frustrating thing is that this land has so much potential. We have millions of barrels under that ground," he says. Opposite the mound is a large, black pipe, marked by yellow wooden poles warning people not to approach. "This is it—the pipeline that goes all the way to Turkey." Thirty inches in diameter, the pipe is designed to carry billions of dollars' worth of oil from Kirkuk. It lies completely exposed—and in these volatile times, vulnerable. Worse, the flow has dried up, and with it, the cash to sustain Kirkuk's economy.

Signs of this strain aren't hard to find. Driving on one of the main roads that leads into downtown Kirkuk, a visitor comes upon a wire fence encircling a few thousand canvas tents. Inside the camp, families of five or more internally displaced Kurds live in tents, clothes hanging on strings that cling to the wooden posts. At night, children lie about on tattered mattresses and women boil water for tea over small fires. Health care is minimal.

Those forced to flee from their homes in Iraq, found themselves living less than four miles away from ISIS encampments, protected only by the Kurdish Peshmerga. If the brutal threat

of ISIS weren't dispiriting enough, the economic nosedive that
arrived in tandem with the oil disaster added another layer of
despair. Thousands here rely on jobs as civil servants to feed
their families, and now they were having to work without pay.

Instead, men line the side of the road in the early mornings,
squatting as they keep an eye out for construction trucks. Some
private companies pick them up if they need extra hands for
the day. Further down the street, in the local schools, children
are packed into consolidated classrooms, fighting for seats
because the teaching staff has been cut. ATM service is also
intermittent on any given day because many machines have not
been restocked with cash. Local restaurants are force to operate
on an "IOU" system.

The fight over Kirkuk is exacerbated by its history of changing
boundaries. Since the discovery of oil in the governorate in
the 1920s, and particularly from the 1960s onward, there have
been continuous attempts to transform the ethnic makeup of
the region. This demographic shift coincided with the governorate's changing boundaries: Kirkuk went from about 20,000
square kilometers in 1950 to less than 10,000 square kilometers
by the turn of the twenty-first century.

The boundaries changed several times after the end of
British rule and continued to arbitrarily shift under the Ba'ath
regime. Saddam detached the Kurdish regions of Chamchamal and Kalar from the governorate; both were incorpo-
rated into Sulaymaniyah. In 2000, the Iraqi government merged
the city of Sargaran into Dibis into Kirkuk province, cleaving

36   it off from Kirkuk and shrinking Kirkuk's population to 1930s levels. Today, the Kirkuk region formally lies outside the official boundaries of Iraqi Kurdistan, while the main Kurdish parties regard it as a viable extension of the KRG. The boundary dispute festers despite avowals by all sides—the Baghdad government, the KRG, and the post-invasion U.S. overseers—that they want to fix it.

The UN boundary of the Kurdistan region is supposed to be the Green Line, the former ceasefire line with the Iraqi army established after the 1991 Kurdish uprising. But the KRG maintains it should not only control the governorates of Dahuk, Erbil, and Sulaimaniya, but also officially control Kirkuk, Diyala, and Ninewa. Baghdad maintains that Diyala and Ninewa belong to Iraq proper, not to Kurdistan.

Enter the Americans. At the U.S.'s urging, the Iraqi Governing Council, the post-invasion government, passed what is known as the Law of the Administration for the State of Iraq for the Transitional Period, or TAL. The council was headed by Ahmed Chalabi and reported directly to the Coalition Provisional Authority, led by Paul Bremer. Ten Americans appointed by the Bush administration helped to draft the law.

It was meant to be an interim document of governance, but a great deal of the TAL was included in the official Iraqi constitution, approved in 2005, which proved controversial, especially in Kurdistan and the disputed provinces. Non-Kurdish minorities felt it favored the Kurds in the ongoing dispute over the Green Line and in the Kurds' push to expand Kurdistan's

boundaries. Locals posted flyers outside mosques criticizing
U.S. influence. One such pamphlet read: "Do not let the occupation forces appoint people to write the constitution. Yes, to
elections and we want a constitution written by Iraqis and with
Iraqi ideas—not foreign."

At the time of the drafting, Arabs and Turkmen, who represented a considerable bulk of Kirkuk's population, were increas-
ingly concerned about the massive Kurdish influx back into the
city. Thousands upon thousands of Kurds who had been driven
out of Kirkuk under Saddam moved back to their homes after
the liberation in March 2003. They then took over key leadership positions in the city. The chief of police was a Kurd, and
so was the governor. Kurds walked around the city writing "For
Sale" on Arab homes, or simply occupied them.

The Kurdish leadership, knowing that the TAL would define
their future, worked closely with several members of the American committee. Among them was Peter Galbraith, a onetime
U.S. diplomat who had signed on as an unpaid advisor to the
Kurdish government. Galbraith was well known in Kurdish cir-
cles for having helped to expose Saddam's gassing of the Kurds
in the late 1980s while serving as a staffer for the Senate Foreign Relations Committee. He traveled on fact finding missions
to investigate Saddam's treatment of the Kurds. He gathered a
collection of documents of evidence of war crimes dating back
to World War II. Galbraith, who favored a three-state solu-
tion for Iraq that would give the Kurds a defined homeland,
didn't divulge at the time that he had acquired an interest in the

CHAPTER ONE – CAPITAL OF THE OIL MIRAGE

production-sharing contract by DNO, a Norwegian oil corporation, just as he was brokering a production and exploration deal between the Kurdish government and DNO.

(The agreement allowed DNO to explore for Kurdish oil and produce that oil without Baghdad's approval. Galbraith later said he thought the deal would help further the cause of Kurdish independence. In 2010, a British court ordered DNO to pay Galbraith and a Yemeni investor between $55 million and $75 million to settle arbitration claims over the much-criticized agreement.)

Whatever its shortcomings, the TAL and the subsequent constitution seemed like documents that might settle the Kurdish boundary disputes. Article 58 of the TAL said the federal government would act "expeditiously to take measures to remedy the injustice caused by the previous regime's practices in altering the demographic character of certain regions, including Kirkuk." It contained provisions to make reparations for Saddam's Anfal atrocities. Those provisions included moving people who had been forcibly displaced by the Ba'ath regime back to their homes, giving them new jobs, and allowing people to determine their own national identity and ethnic affiliation.

As to the internal borders, Article 58 empowered the Presidency Council of the Iraqi Transitional Government, a body chosen by the National Assembly, to make recommendations on remedying border changes imposed on disputed territories, and the territorial settlements would be deferred until reparations for the Anfal campaign were carried out and a census conducted.

Alas, as Fouad Hussein tells me over and over again, little has come of any of this. The Kurds are still pressing for the federal government to implement Article 140 of the 2005 constitution, which is the constitution's analogy to the TAL's Article 58. Article 140 contains provisions for the resolution of the status of not only Kirkuk but of all of the disputed territories. The article establishes a three-stage process of normalization, census, and referendum. If Article 140 is implemented, it would help determine who holds the rights to the massive oil fields in Kirkuk. Article 140 envisioned a referendum on the status of Kirkuk by the end of 2007. But ten years later the article is still delayed.

Baghdad and Erbil interpret the constitution differently. Most constitutional analysts say the central government has the right to manage all existing fields, and the provincial governments have the right to oversee new fields. The KRG often cites the constitutional provision that outlines that argument, Article 112. The article says Baghdad's dominion over oil and gas applies only to "present fields." In the Kurdish administration's view, this means new oil and gas finds in Kurdish territory belong to and ought to be managed by the KRG. Baghdad has doggedly taken an opposing view. As a result, numerous Western companies were reluctant to contract with the Kurds, not wishing to upset Baghdad, with whom they also do business. Former Iraqi oil minister Hussain al-Shahristani often threatened to blacklist any oil company that did business directly with the Kurdish government and its companies.

All this was still being disputed in 2014 when ISIS rolled in and seized huge swaths of northern Iraq. The Kurdish military

40   took over oil fields previously run by the North Oil Company, claiming they were defending them from ISIS after the Iraqi army had left. But Baghdad viewed Erbil's seizure as simply an illegal takeover. (North Oil Company was still in control of Baba Gurgur).

"Kirkuk is the richest place for oil and it has the poorest people," says Hussein. "The money has not been invested in creating business centers or establishing infrastructure projects. The government has failed us!"

The Wizard of Oil

Those who know Ashti Hawrami well tend to like him. He's said to be amiable, even grandfatherly. "When you meet him, he comes off as a sweet old man," says one person who has known him for more than a decade.

Hawrami was what some in the oil industry and in the Kurdish government called a "master of contract negotiations." Part of what made Hawrami "a wizard," as one parliamentarian put it to me, was his knowledge of the industry and his ability to implement contracts that helped the ministry reap maximum rewards. The structure of the contracts themselves is important to the story of how the oil business developed in Kurdistan. But the language surrounding contracts is dry and filled with industry jargon. So, let's look at a scenario most people would understand. While this might not be the most technical description of oil contracts in the KRG, it will help most get an idea of how they work.

Let's say there's an international corporation called Citron that's in the business of selling orange juice around the world. Citron asks the town of Sunnyville, which has some of the largest orchards on its land, if it can pick its oranges to make juice. Sunnyville would like a local business to make the harvest, but unfortunately none of them have the capacity or the resources to do so. So, Sunnyville sets out some specific terms for Citron to follow.

First, the government of Sunnyville maintains ownership of the orchards and works with third-party traders to sell the juice on the market. Second, Citron will only be given access to part of the orchards, a grove on the east side of town. Third, Citron needs to invest up front in things like storage containers for the oranges, harvesting tools, and water pipes for irrigation. Sunnyville promises that it will pay back Citron's investment once the town gets its money from the sale of the juice.

For Citron, working with these terms is worth it if it can get access to a sizeable grove that yields great oranges, and Sunnyville sees Citron's proposal as a fantastic opportunity to boost its economy. So the two parties draw up a contract and negotiate terms, which is as follows: Sunnyville gets a 10 percent royalty fee up front for letting Citron in; after Citron is reimbursed for infrastructure investments and deducts operating costs of 10 percent, Sunnyville, as the landlord, gets 50 percent of the remaining profits as rent for owning the orchards. Only then do Sunnyville and Citron split the rest 20-80.

On top all of that, Citron also promises to pay the Sunny-   43
ville government bonuses which go into funds that are supposed to help pay for things like playgrounds and parks.

And knowing that not every grove produces oranges,
Sunnyville tells Citron that the company is responsible for the
financial burden if the trees die. But if the grove is successful,
Sunnyville needs to pay its share of the forward development
costs.

The two parties sign the contract and get to work, and soon
enough, oranges are ready to be picked and made into juice.
Once the juice is processed, it ships to buyers across the world,
and Citron starts to make money.

Let's say for our purposes that the orange juice venture in
Sunnyville makes $100 for the first round of sales. The govern-
ment claims its 10 percent royalty fee, or $10. Citron had put in
$50 in upfront costs, and Sunnyville promised to repay Citron
for those costs. So, Citron takes $50 out of the remaining $90
and puts it back into its bank account. Then it deducts $10 in
operating costs. That leaves $30 of remaining profits. As land-
lord, Sunnyville gets 50 percent of that amount as rent, or $15.
That leaves $15. Sunnyville gets another 20 percent, or $3 while
Citron gets the remaining 80 percent, or $12.

The scenario described is similar to what is called a production-sharing agreement. PSAs were first used in Indonesia
in the 1960s, at a time of growing nationalism. Under a PSA,
the state, as the owner of natural resources, engages a foreign

44   company as a contractor to provide technical services, financial support, operational control, and management expertise for exploration and development operations. The state is traditionally represented by the government or one of its entities, such as the national oil company. In the case of the Kurdish contracts, the Ministry of Natural Resources represented the government.

The other kind of contract, the one used by the Ministry of Oil in Baghdad, is a technical service agreement. A company essentially works for the national oil company for a set period of time. The company does not own any of the oil it produces, but it gets a fixed fee per barrel, which is paid after reimbursement of the costs it incurs. Part of the reason Baghdad uses TSAs is because the fields in the south are already developed. There is hardly any oil exploration needed in that part of the country, and the government is more comfortable with its knowledge of its resources.

PSAs are different from other types of oil contracts because the foreign company carries much of the risk. If it doesn't find oil, it doesn't get any compensation. Under PSAs, instead of the company paying the state government for the oil it takes, the government compensates the company for its investment and operational costs once a field is commercial. When an oil company enters a country to explore and produce oil, it invests up front in things like drilling operations, storage containers, and pipelines. The company invests with the assurance, via contracts, that it will get repaid with an offsetting share of the oil later.

The company is entitled to recover the costs of development once sales start. The company takes back what it put forward in the beginning, as well as ongoing operational costs. The balance of the profit is split among the government and the company. However, before the profit is split, the Kurdish government takes a royalty, as well as agreed bonuses, both signatory and others. Some of the bonuses include cash payments that were to be set aside for things like infrastructure projects.

Many of the contracts signed before Hawrami entered office did not have extensive cash bonuses attached to them. They did, however, have signatory bonuses. When Hawrami entered the Ministry of Natural Resources, he implemented terms that allowed the government to tack on cash payments that went directly to the government. Many of those payments were supposedly destined for things like hospitals, roads, and bridge maintenance, but Western oil companies rarely followed up on the final destination of those funds. Hawrami was a master negotiator. Many oil executives described him as a "wheeler and dealer."

The Kurdish government did not negotiate the same terms with each international oil company, which is not unusual. And after the first set of deals, Hawrami and the ministry renegotiated contracts, sometimes on a whim, according to a study of court documents and emails between the ministry and executives. With some, Hawrami was willing to give greater tax breaks or more favorable payouts, especially for firms that invested first or made certain commitments. Some companies simply have to pay a 5 percent tax, while others were required to pay much more.

These lucrative contracts led many Kurds to praise Hawrami, saying he brought the natural resource wealth back to the people. Others disagreed, claiming the minister contributed to the system that allowed politicians to profit handsomely from the oil sector while ordinary Kurds suffered.

Hawrami created a system requiring bonuses from the oil companies as a condition of doing business. These bonuses, in some form, are in natural resource contracts across the world. The problem with the bonuses, though, is that no one in the KRG besides the Ministry of Natural Resources knows where the funds sit, according to officials in the finance ministry. The lack of transparency makes it hard to tell if the funds meant for infrastructure projects and other public programs are going to the right places. Investigators in the U.S., the UK, and elsewhere described these bonuses as a part of the ministry's "pay-to-play" scheme. Other parts of that scheme included more direct payments in the form of, for example, armored cars.

Those who believed in him said Hawrami took control and created a strong front that could fight back against Baghdad in oil disputes. From an outsider's perspective, the minister was a good salesman who was able to sign up internationally reputable companies to use as leverage in the fight for more Kurdish autonomy.

The Atrush block is an oilfield that lies near the top of Iraqi Kurdistan, north of Mosul. Industry estimates pegged the block as a potential gusher, one of the largest in the region. But the importance of Atrush actually has to do not with the quantity of oil it yields, but with its location. It sits next to the prized jewel Shaikan block and analysts say part of Atrush

connects to Shaikan. Hawrami knew it would get the attention
of foreign firms.

In 2007, an American firm called Aspect Energy International wanted a piece of the budding Kurdistan oil sector.
Aspect's move was to acquire General Exploration Partners,
a Cayman Islands company that owned 80 percent of the
Atrush license, with the Kurdish government holding on to
the remainder. Then, prior to a special meeting in 2010, Aspect
picked up a mysterious new partner, selling one third of its stake
in GEP to an entity called ShaMaran Petroleum for $24.1 million
and 12.5 million ShaMaran shares.

ShaMaran's lineage traces to a tiny Canadian mining, oil,
and gas exploration firm called Kit Resources that ran an operating loss of about $1 million in 2006, and had total assets of
less than $3 million. Then in 2007, Kit changed its name to
Bayou Bend Petroleum and hired as its Chief Operating Officer
a man with deep ties to Hawrami and the Kurdish government
who had been a general manager of an oil firm in the region.
According to investigators in the U.S. and the UK, Bayou Bend
dumped its assets on a Swedish oil company (whose owners had
sat on the Kit Resources board) and others—including individ-
uals working for the Kurdish government, who had acquired
some 150 million shares.

A company letter to shareholders prior to the special
meeting in 2010 announced that Bayou Bend's prospects had
greatly improved since its Kit Resources days, and now included
substantial agreements with the Kurdish government to develop oil and gas fields there. "Iraqi-Kurdistan . . . is estimated

48 to contain up to 45 billion of Iraq's 115 billion barrels of oil reserves," the company's CEO, Keith Hill, wrote in the letter. "The Kirkuk field . . . is one of the world's largest, containing reserves of over 20 billion barrels of oil. The area is highly underexplored and is currently undergoing a massive exploration and development campaign by over 30 mid- to large-size international oil companies."

At the special meeting, "to better reflect the Corporation's new focus in Kurdistan," the letter continues, another name change was proposed. "ShaMaran is a local Kurdish deity reflecting wisdom and secrets." Hill's letter also said ShaMaran's board was asking shareholders to approve the issuance of another 250 million common shares.

ShaMaran, according to investigators, was merely the vehicle by which the Kurdish government could feed oil contracts to companies owned by its Kurdistan colleagues, while pocketing millions of dollars in "bonuses" that the firms had to pay to sign Kurdish government oil contracts. Investigators said that Hawrami simply leveraged his insider position to use other oil companies' finds in neighboring fields to entice more investors to pour millions of dollars into ShaMaran stock, running up the share price.

"All investors in ShaMaran could see was that they were in a known oil block," says one of the investigators. "Hence it was easy to hoodwink shareholders to buy shares." Kurdish government insiders who held millions of ShaMaran shares unloaded them near the peak of the market at $1.48 a share, making fortunes for themselves, according to documents supplied by the investigators.

The ShaMaran deal keeps on paying off for the Kurdish government. In 2013, Aspect sold its interest to the Emirati oil corporation TAQA for $600 million. Kurdish government insiders personally took in millions in fees from the sale, according to investigators.

Years of secret wheeling and dealing gradually began making trouble for Hawrami, and he faced a few close calls. In 2008, the Oslo Stock Exchange investigated a transaction of shares of the Norwegian oil company DNO and accused it of insider trading, after the bourse found that the transaction had been brokered by the Kurdish government through an account registered to Hawrami, who was also a shareholder in DNO. The shares were sold to Turkish firm Genel Enerji, which subsequently sold them to another company called RAK Petroleum. The Kurdish government suspended DNO's operations in Kurdistan and levied a large fine, to the dismay of the company. The bourse eventually dropped the charge of insider trading, but DNO's share price plummeted. RAK then took the opportunity to build further stakes in DNO, eventually taking it over in 2010.

Hawrami claimed he and other officials had not profited personally from the dealing of shares, though investigators with a regulatory enforcement group in the UK said they have evidence that disputed the claim. The investigators said that they

50   sent the evidence up the chain of command, but that nothing ever came of it.

In the same year as the DNO scandal, the UK's Financial Services Authority said that Hawrami received emails from Ian Hannam, then J.P. Morgan's global chairman of equity capital markets, that contained information about a potential takeover bid of Heritage Oil, which Hannam was also working for as an advisor. Hawrami instructed brokers to buy $21 million in Heritage shares on behalf of the Kurdish government—but the FSA investigation concluded that Hannam's emails did not inform that decision. The FSA ended up going after Hannam and fining him for insider trading.

Several times over the course of 2016, I tried to contact Hawrami's office by phone and email to set up an interview with him and with executives at the KAR Group, what many call the de facto Kurdistan national oil company. No one in the ministry or KAR responded to my requests. In Erbil, toward the end of my reporting trip in August of 2016, I decided I would drop in on KAR to see who might be willing to speak to me.

I had interviewed a Kurdish security official in charge of guarding the KAR compound and surrounding oil fields, and he told me a visit to KAR headquarters would be fine. But it was not a warm welcome. I encountered a somewhat bemused manager who spoke perfect English. "I can't tell you anything and I can't show you anything. I just made a call to the ministry and I have been instructed not to talk to you. Without Mr. Ashti's approval, I cannot do anything for you."

This seemed somewhat odd given that Hawrami's office had emailed me earlier to say he would, in fact, sit down with me. So we showed up at the massive gates of the Ministry of Natural Resources in downtown Erbil at the appointed time. We were shown in by a short, thin man with a blue blazer who only identified himself as Omed. Omed had disappointing news for us.

"The minister has reconsidered your request," he said. "I know you think this story is important, but it will have no impact on us."

All in the Family

One explanation for government failure in Iraqi Kurdistan is that government itself isn't what it seems to be. Here, politics, business, and family are inseparable. Two rival families, the Barzanis and the Talabanis, rule the two main political parties and call most of the shots. If oil hasn't proved a blessing to the people of Kurdistan, it's certainly been extremely lucrative for the Barzanis and Talabanis, their friends, and their business associates.

The Kurdistan Democratic Party has historically been dominated by the Barzani tribe, with origins in the Badinan region of Iraqi Kurdistan's territory in northern Iraq. The KDP was led by Mullah Mustafa Barzani, whose heroic stand as a resistance fighter against successive Baghdad governments and whose drive for Kurdish independence remain legendary in Kurdish history. The KDP's current leader is his surviving son, Masoud Barzani. Masoud's deputy and nephew—some say, probable heir—is Nechirvan Barzani, the prime minister of the Kurdistan region. Many Barzani family members hold high positions in the government—Masoud's eldest son heads the intelligence service, and his two brothers are leaders in the KDP's Peshmerga. The Barzanis have come to own or control a number of interlocking Kurdistan companies that do business in practically every commercial sector, including oil and energy.

The other main party, the Patriotic Union of Kurdistan, broke away from the KDP in 1975. The PUK is dominated by the Talabani family, led by Jalal Talabani, the first non-Arab president of Iraq, until his death in October 2017. One of Jalal's sons is the deputy prime minister, and the other is a leader of the PUK and its military forces.

Critics have long accused both the KDP and the PUK of corruption, nepotism, and cronyism, in part for keeping thousands of party members on the public payroll. The parties and the leading families compete for business contracts, including deals in the energy industry. They force foreign oil developers to pay local companies as consultants—companies that are almost always linked to the KDP or the PUK, who kick hefty "consultation fees" back to the families so they can fund their parties. The scheme has become widely known, and was thoroughly described in a 2006 U.S. State Department cable made public by WikiLeaks in 2014. "The real godfathers never reveal themselves," the cable states. "If anyone tries to cause one of their companies a problem or take away a contract, the godfathers just say, 'That belongs to a cousin of mine' and the matter is dropped."

The State Department specifically called out the two ruling parties, claiming they facilitated the corruption and profited handsomely off of it. "The core of the corruption . . . lies with those who control the security forces. They keep the game running because controlling the guns means they can enforce their illegal contracts," the cable states. "Security forces, and thus corruption networks, depend on their patrons and thus seldom cross party lines." Companies like the Diyar Group, Eagle Group, KAR Group, and Falcon Group, according to investigators, are connected to one or more of the leaders in the two ruling families.

For example, Jalal Talabani was known to set up deals through small firms with connections to him or his sons. Of the U.S. companies winning Kurdish contracts, the first to strike a deal was a firm called Prime Natural Resources, based out of Houston. Prime's CEO, Richard Anderson, was an experienced oil patch hand. Anderson met Talabani, who had already awarded production-sharing contracts to Genel Enerji, an established Turkish oil giant, and PetOil, a relatively small explorer that owned refineries and transported oil across the Turkish border. PetOil needed a partner to shoulder some of the risk of operating in this volatile region, and cash for exploration.

PetOil reached out to Talabani's son Bafel, who, according to documents that surfaced in a later British court case, arranged for Prime Natural Resources to obtain a 50 percent stake in the PetOil contract. According to investigators, Bafel set up the meeting with Anderson with the understanding that Prime's involvement wouldn't be disclosed—and so that the Talabanis' cut of the deal wouldn't be known.

"Many party leaders do not see what they do as wrong. They think of it as just compensation for all their sacrifices in the struggle. The second tier of leaders in the KDP and PUK politburos below Barzani and Talabani also participate in the corruption," the cable concludes. Corruption is Kurdistan's biggest economic problem, singlehandedly stalling the growth of the entire regional economy. But the state department still offers a glimmer of hope: "[T]he third generation of leaders divides between those who want their turn at the trough and those who want to end corruption."

A six-day trial in the case of Monde Petroleum SA v. Westernzagros Ltd. in June 2016 cast a damning light on this "godfather" system and how Kurdistan's ruling elite use their family names and political connections to cash in on Kurdistan's oil and gas wealth.

Westernzagros was a subsidiary of Western Oil Sands International, whose principal business is a 20 percent interest in an oil sands project in the western Canadian province of Alberta. In 2004 and 2005, Western Oil Sands signed memoranda of understanding with Baghdad to undertake exploratory work in the Kurdish region. But in 2006, as the politics on the ground began to shift, it independently reached an exploration contract with the KRG. Westernzagros would do the actual exploration and drilling, but under pressure from KRG operatives, Westernzagros had to bring in a local, connected company as a consultant, presumably to negotiate a production-sharing contract in the region of Sulaymaniyah, a mountainous governorate

56 in western Kurdistan that is controlled by the Patriotic Union of Kurdistan, the party presided over by the Talabani clan. The company that was chosen was Monde Petroleum, an oil venture run by Yassir Al-Fekaiki, the son of a former opposition leader in the Iraqi National Congress, and a business partner of Talabani's son Bafel.

In June 2006, Hawrami stepped into his role as the Minister of Natural Resources, and he considered the terms negotiated before he took office too generous, including Westernzagros's deal. Using his wizardry, Hawrami managed to reduce Westernzagros's exploratory acreage by about 40 percent of what was initially agreed upon; the company had little choice but to ratify the agreement. On top of the diminished acreage, Hawrami imposed terms intended to cut well-connected Kurds in on the action (which had been happening even before his time as minister), and spin off more oil cash into KRG coffers.

Under the new agreement, Monde would get monthly fees, bonuses upon completion of a set of milestones, plus an option to acquire a 3 percent interest in any production-sharing contract they landed for Westernzagros. This wasn't chump change. A 2014 regulatory filing put the value of Westernzagros's 40 percent share of an estimated 500 million barrels in its ongoing Kurdistan operations at $1.5 billion, and the fields covered by the agreement could hold another billion barrels of oil. According to Al-Fekaiki, he would also receive a $700,000 "consultation fee," with much of that sum actually going to Talabani.

To Al-Fekaiki's surprise, however, that didn't seem to be sufficient for Talabani. Behind the scenes, the "godfather" was maneuvering Westernzagros to sign a new agreement with a company controlled by the Talabani family and the PUK. According to Al-Fekaiki, Talabani claimed that Westernzagros would be willing to indirectly share revenues with Monde so long as Al-Fekaiki agreed to terminate the agreement. If he refused, Westernzagros would withhold the $700,000 consulting payment. Al-Fekaiki agreed, and records show that Westernzagros then sent the $700,000 payment to Monde. Al-Fekaiki claimed that 75 percent of it went into Talibani's pocket, though people affiliated with Monde denied the payment ever went through.

Al-Fekaiki soon realized he would *not* be sharing any profits, and in 2013 he brought suit against Westernzagros in the English High Court, claiming the company and Talabani used falsehoods to get him to terminate his agreement. Monde also commenced arbitration proceedings before the International Chamber of Commerce as a protective measure, but the tribunal determined that it had no jurisdiction over the case.

Hawrami's brand of complicated and confusing production-sharing agreements make this kind of double-crossing and court disputes common. "Sharing agreements means there are many, many discussions between the government and company about what they are going to share. They fight about anything and everything," says Jenik Radon, a professor at Columbia's School for International and Public Affairs, himself an experienced international oil contract negotiator. "This happens all over the world. For example, Saudi Arabia passed a law in saying if you want to do business there you need a local intermediate

58   that is approved by the Saudi government. You have to pay the local intermediate 10 percent of every deal."

Al-Fekaiki told the court that such payments were "re-cast" in contractual documents to get around bribery laws in the West, but they were in fact "nothing more than kickbacks for local politicians." The judge found that Al-Fekaiki and Talabani were both trying to cheat Westernzagros and squeeze as much money as they could from the contract, though he did not view Westernzagros in any more favorable light, deeming it a willing participant—an apt characterization of many Western energy companies that were playing along and skirting bribery laws. Furthermore, the judge ruled that Westernzagros, working with Talabani, had indeed used misrepresentation to induce Monde to terminate its contract, but that Westernzagros actually had the right to terminate the agreement because Monde had not met certain performance milestones as laid out in the contract. Damages to Monde were denied. It was clear that there were no winners in the case.

None, that is, except for Hawrami and Talabani, the "real godfathers" who "never reveal themselves," as the WikiLeaks cable pertinently noted—they were not even parties or witnesses in the suit. Unfortunately, the enrichment of these "godfathers" augurs bad days for anyone who might want Kurdistan's oil wealth to actually be tapped. Kickbacks to the Barzanis and Talabanis in the form of consultation fees and contract renegotiations means that the clans are rewarded whether or not a single drop of oil is pumped from the ground. As Westernzagros CEO Simon Hatfield once lamented, "all it does is cost us fruitless money and delays the development of the region."

Here Comes
the West

Rex Wempen slowly wiped the raindrops that began to gather on the end of his nose. By the night of March 19, 2003, he had walked for days, slumping up rocks that jutted out from the mountainside. It rarely stopped misting as he walked, making it difficult for his feet to grip the ground. Because the Turkish border was closed, he had hired Kurdish smugglers to guide him through a pass in the Alborz Mountains that separates northern Iran from Kurdish Iraq.

Wempen had served in the U.S. Army in the first Gulf War, and he was returning to Iraq just as U.S. President George W. Bush was about to make good on his threats to wage another Gulf War to remove Saddam Hussein from power. Two days earlier, Bush had told a national television audience: "It is too late for Saddam Hussein to remain in power. It is not too late for the Iraqi military to act with honor and protect your country by permitting the peaceful entry of coalition forces to eliminate

60   weapons of mass destruction. Our forces will give Iraqi military units clear instructions on actions they can take to avoid being attacked and destroyed. I urge every member of the Iraqi military and intelligence services, if war comes, do not fight for a dying regime that is not worth your own life."

This was a war that had been in the making since Wempen's previous time in Iraq. As Operation Desert Storm came to an end in 1991, it became clear that Saddam would remain in power. Zalmay Khalilzad, then a deputy undersecretary for policy planning in the Department of Defense, emerged as an influential voice who believed the U.S. should be doing more to stop Hussein from committing more massacres. Khalilzad was among the drafters of the 1992 Defense Planning Guidance, which became a blueprint of how the U.S. could maintain its status in the world going forward. With the collapse of the Soviet Union, the U.S. needed to prevent the rise of another peer competitor, and Khalilzad believed the best way to do so was to invest in Iraq. If the government got involved with Baghdad, Khalilzad thought, it could capitalize economically on the country's massive oil reserves, even if the oil infrastructure in the country was old and in need of repair. The DPG document said the American objective in the Middle East and Southwest Asia "is to remain the predominant outside power in the region and preserve U.S. and Western access to the region's oil."

After reading the DPG, Dick Cheney, then the Secretary of Defense, told Khalilzad: "You've discovered a new rationale for our role in the world. I read the document last night and I think it is brilliant." Paul Wolfowitz, the deputy secretary of defense on policy, also aligned with Khalilzad, and advocated for intervening in Iraq.

Khalilzad, however, would later write in his book, *The Envoy*, that the war in Iraq did not materialize from the DPG document. "It is true that many of the DPG's far-reaching and controversial ideas were gradually adopted as U.S. policy under both the Clinton and George W. Bush administrations," Khalilzad wrote. "The notion that the 1992 DPG presaged the Iraq War, however, ignores a more fundamental reality: It was the 9/11 attack, not any earlier history, that explains the decision to invade Iraq."

Indeed, plans for a war in Iraq moved quickly following September 11. In March of 2002, the State Department undertook a policy-development initiative called "The Future of Iraq Project," where more than two hundred experts were charged with coming up with strategies on things like public health, education, economy, anti-corruption, and oil and energy. The Oil and Energy Working Group's final report said: "Iraq should be opened to international oil companies as quickly as possible after the war . . . the country should establish a conducive business environment to attract investment in oil and gas reserves."

However, there is evidence that the George W. Bush administration planned for the invasion of Iraq well before 9/11, often with oil in mind. Former Treasury Secretary Paul O'Neill said that Vice President Cheney wanted the U.S. to intervene in Iraq before the terrorist attacks, according to Ron Suskind's book *The Price of Loyalty*. In early 2001, Cheney set up an Energy Task Force in the administration to consult with energy executives on ways to expand American investment overseas. As

62   first reported by *The New Yorker* in 2004, a secret document, written by a top National Security Council official, directed the NSC staff to cooperate with the Energy Task Force, "as it considered the 'melding' of two seemingly unrelated areas of policy: 'the review of operational policies towards rogue states,' such as Iraq, and 'actions regarding the capture of new and existing oil and gas fields.'"

Cheney and the White House blocked Congress from learning even the most basic information about the task force's activities, according to National Security Archive documents. But in 2003, the U.S. Department of Commerce, responding to a FOIA request from Judicial Watch, a conservative government watchdog group, released a 2001 map produced by the task force that showed the extent to which it had laid it out its vision for American-led oil development in Iraq, particularly in Iraqi Kurdistan. It detailed its plan down to the division of Kurdistan oil and gas blocks, including which countries claimed exploration rights and which blocks were still up for grabs. One document names different countries from Algeria to Italy to China. Under each country's name was the name of a firm representing the country in negotiations, the blocks that the country were bidding on, and the status of the negotiations. Russia and Canada had put in the largest number of bids in Iraq—twelve bids at twelve different locations.

Britain undertook its own postmortem of the war with the Iraq Inquiry hearings. Jonny Baxter, the head of the Department for International Development office in Iraq from October 2007 to May 2008, testified that the UK and the U.S. worked closely

together on the ground, especially when it came to unlocking
the country's natural resources. "Our top line really was to help
Iraq unlock its own resources, to make use of its own resources
and to effectively turn those into services for the Iraqi people,"
he said during his testimony. "That involved helping the Iraqis
have the sort of leadership capacity to achieve that. So at a sort
of high level, that was what we were going in to do."

Ties between the Bush administration and the U.S. oil and
gas industry were well known. One of Bush's closest friends,
Ray Hunt, was one of the first high-profile oilmen to sign a deal
with the Kurdistan Regional Government. Hunt was a member
of the National Petroleum Council, an industry organization that advises the Secretary of Energy, and he served as its
chairman from June 1991 to July 1994. Many oil executives were
privy to the government's discussions about Iraq's oil prospects
and the possibility of intervention.

According to current and former American and British
financial regulatory enforcement officers, Rex Wempen was one
of those people.

Wempen thought of himself as a doer, and saw military service
as a portal to his ambitions. A tall, muscular man with thinning
hair, he'd grown up in Rancho Palos Verdes, an affluent suburb of
Los Angeles, with a family deeply connected to the Republican
elite in Washington. His father and brother had both served in
the military.

Wempen attended Cornell University on an Army reserves
scholarship and played middle linebacker on Cornell's football

64   team. He went on to Georgetown's National Security Studies Program, and in 1989 entered the Foreign Service, later working for two U.S. congressmen. The Army recalled him to active duty during the first Gulf War, and he served as a special forces team leader with the Green Berets, rising to the rank of captain. He also received top-secret security clearance.

After the war, Wempen enrolled in an MBA program at the University of Southern California. But after an incident at a nightclub where he wrestled with another reservist on a lawn at 2:00 a.m., the police charged him with disturbing the peace. The Army discharged him from the reserves after he was accused of forging signatures on a disciplinary document involving another soldier.

From November 2002 to February 2003, Wempen worked as a consultant to a company called Pivotal Ventures, "advising them on counter-terrorism applications for their technology and supporting their federal government marketing efforts by briefing high level Pentagon officers," he said. Court documents show Wempen maintained his top-secret security clearance despite the fact that he had been discharged unfavorably. Two months after he left Pivotal, he established his own firm, Excalibur. The company was only a nameplate without shareholders or a board of directors.

Wempen's goal was simple: Get into Kurdistan ahead of the hordes of Western oil prospectors who would be trying to get in as well. He was just one of many with the same thought. Dozens of small-time businesses all wanted in to what they expected would become a burgeoning oil contractor market, and they all courted the Kurdish government. While Kurdistan held just a small percentage of the overall reserves in Iraq, there was ample opportunity. Wempen would eventually become a small fish in a very big sea. It was common knowledge in the industry that the Kurds were keen to develop their oilfields, and vast riches potentially awaited those with the nerve and connections to get there first. Wempen had wrangled all the right connections.

Days before Operation Iraqi Freedom began, Wempen flew into Ankara, Turkey's capital, to meet Hoshyar Zebari, a leader in the Kurdistan Democratic Party and the uncle of KDP President Masoud Barzani. Zebari wanted to talk about investment in Kurdistan. Wempen, over tea in a Turkish government conference room, was all ears. He told Zebari that he wanted to be one of the first U.S. businessman in line. Some Western companies had carved out Iraq oil prospects as far back as the 1950s. At the time of the beginning of the war, the Chinese and Russians had eaten up parts of the oil industry in southern Iraq. But everyone who had followed the region's oil fortunes knew everything would be reset after the fall of Saddam.

In the same room in Ankara was Zalmay Khalilzad, who had become the go-to guy for setting up meetings between Iraqi and American officials and potential Western energy investors. It was said that if you were on Khalilzad's good side, you had a sure chance of signing Iraqi oil contracts. Wempen's view was that his lack of experience in the oil industry could be overcome by leveraging the right connections, and he scoffed at advice from a friend to go slow. He was eager to play for big stakes.

66   On March 20, 2003, U.S. ground forces invaded Iraq, and Operation Iraqi Freedom commenced. That same day, Wempen reached Erbil. Zebari, who had become Iraqi Kurdistan's foreign relations representative, held off setting up formal conferences until after the fall of Saddam's regime. In the meantime, Wempen was under the protection of several Kurdish Peshmerga bodyguards as he attempted to conduct business in a chaotic Iraq. He set up shop under his Excalibur nameplate in Erbil's Ishtar Sheraton Hotel, traveling back and forth between Kurdistan and Baghdad despite the danger of crossing a country under invasion.

Wempen leveraged his position as one of the first on the ground to clinch consulting gigs with various companies looking to invest in the country. He helped set up the Iraq branch of a U.S. firm called Diligence to provide intelligence and security, was hired as a consultant by Occidental Petroleum to help them land a KRG deal, and won a contract to conduct something called the National Economic Survey of Iraq. He tried to set up something called the Iraq Recovery Fund, which would encourage and help U.S. companies wanting to invest in Iraqi energy and infrastructure projects. He even established the Iraq branch of the U.S. Chamber of Commerce.

Problem was, Wempen had no expertise in any of these projects, and they would all fizzle out. By the time he lost the confidence of Zebari, his early benefactor, Wempen's failures had also attracted the negative attention of Ashti Hawrami. By the end of 2004, Wempen realized that it was necessary to have another local partner if he wanted to get anywhere.

Excalibur signed a Memorandum of Understanding with   67
the Dabin Group, a Kurdish investment development company, and it looked for a while as if this would pay off. In 2005,
Wempen received a letter from the soon-to-be Prime Minister
of the Kurdistan Regional Government, Nechirvan Barzani, with
whom the Dabin Group had close links. Barzani invited Wempen
to Erbil to discuss investment opportunities, as the Kurdish government was interested in attracting American capital. Barzani
referred Wempen to George Yacu, his senior oil and gas advisor.
(Yacu, a Kurd who served in Saddam's Ministry of Oil for thirty
years, is now oil-and-gas adviser to Kurdistan's government.)

Yacu suggested the best way for Excalibur to proceed would
be to bring in an independent oil company to operate on a petroleum block together. His partner would have to be American
because the Kurdish government wanted to be seen awarding
concessions to U.S. companies. At that time, Excalibur claimed
it was the petroleum representative of the Shaw Group, a development partner of the giant U.S. corporation Halliburton. The
problem is, it wasn't. Wempen continually lied about Excalibur's
abilities and employee history, as court documents show. At
times, the company said that it had access to a massive network
of petroleum professionals and private equity sources in the U.S.
and worldwide. At other times the company said it was managed
by "highly qualified professionals who brought in rich and diverse
experience in managing investments." None of this was true.

By June, Wempen wrote to Yacu on behalf of Excalibur
requesting an oil concession, preferably on a Kurdistan block that
showed promise. But Excalibur still hadn't secured a U.S. partner.

68 Wempen remembered an acquaintance he'd met in 2003, who picked up the phone and rang Ali Al-Qabandi, a rich and influential Kuwaiti, who was well acquainted with the elite Al-Qassimi family, one of the six ruling clans of the United Arab Emirates who deal in oil through a firm called GIBCA. The Al-Qassimis govern one of the poorest emirates in the UAE, Ras Al-Khaimah, and they wanted to get more involved in the oil industry. Sheikh Sultan Bin Saqr Al-Qassimi had known from his time working at GIBCA that the oil market in Iraqi Kurdistan was growing, and he was put in charge of the efforts to expand operations there. Al-Qassimi and GIBCA had enjoyed a relationship with oil giant ExxonMobil since 1984, partnering to produce lubricants, greases, and other specialty products, but ExxonMobil was not interested in Kurdistan at the time, as global conglomerates are generally risk-averse, and they thought the region was years away from being stable enough to do business in. But Al-Qassimi thought another, much smaller U.S. firm would be the perfect partner for Wempen—especially since it was one that his family was invested in.

Brothers Frank and Todd Kozel ran a company called Texas Keystone, which over the years had gone from a tiny wildcatting operation to a corporation with $40 million in revenues by 2006. They had gained valuable experience, drilling about twelve hundred wells and overseeing fields with eight hundred active wells. In late 1999, the Kozels had branched out, founding Gulf Keystone Petroleum with Al-Qabandi and Al-Qassimi's GIBCA. Al-Qabandi had even become Gulf Keystone's vice president for business development.

The Kozels were still waiting for a big break in the Middle East. The Kozels, Al-Qabandi told Wempen, would be perfect partners for Excalibur. Todd Kozel invited Wempen to a meeting in Tampa, Florida, three days before Christmas in 2005.

Over a ninety-minute lunch at a local restaurant situated on a backwater road, Wempen gave Kozel his Kurdistan spiel, telling him of the Taq Taq and Tawke fields, where oil had been discovered four decades earlier. Both had good flow rates. And then there was the Shaikan block, which geologists had predicted had massive reserves but was still unexplored. Many companies looking into the KRG at this time wanted one thing—Shaikan.

But Taq Taq was, in Wempen's view, underexploited and an easier get. It could be had, but only if Kozel was willing to move quickly. Competition in Kurdistan had grown fierce. Even better, said Wempen, the Kurds were giving preferable treatment to U.S. oil companies. Excalibur and Texas Keystone would make a winning partnership.

Kozel, however, didn't take a shine to Wempen, who was loud and aggressive, his promoter side on full display. Kozel, the youngest brother in his family, was a straight shooter who was quiet, spoke slowly, and didn't like confrontation. Still, he was intrigued by what Wempen had to say.

Wempen, meanwhile, was raring to go. Within two hours, Excalibur had sent a joint venture agreement to Kozel to sign. It was unclear from the contract, however, how the joint venture would treat Gulf and Texas Keystone. On the back end of the deal, Texas Keystone took a 5 percent interest that would

70   transfer to Gulf Keystone under a trust. Wempen maintained that, in a closed-door meeting with Kozel, he had been told he would have a stake in that 5 percent interest; he was never told that the stake was actually intended for Gulf Keystone, to then share with Ashti Hawrami and Masoud Barzani directly.

In the weeks following, Wempen grew impatient when he did not hear back from Kozel on the contract. Meanwhile, Kozel was in Florida for Christmas with his family and awaiting the birth of his second child. Wempen, throughout January, urged Kozel to sign the document several times. The contract went through several negotiations, with amendments addressing things like the split in equity and the ability of each to bring on local partners.

Kozel became more and more wary of his would-be partner. From the very beginning, Hawrami had doubts about Wempen, because of his temperament and lack of oil and gas experience. He may have provided an introduction to the Kozels, but beyond that, Hawrami didn't see a need for Excalibur to stay in on the deal. In fact, according to press reports several years after the deal, Hawrami had specifically asked Kozel to get rid of Wempen.

Although Wempen had wanted Taq Taq, he quickly realized after a site visit to Erbil that the field had already been allocated. Shaikan, then, became the main focus. Eventually, the KRG signed a contract for the Shaikan block with Texas Keystone, Gulf Keystone, and another firm. Gulf Keystone later signed three other contracts for exploration and production in the region.

Gulf Keystone and other companies eventually grew into a network of interrelated businesses that dominated the Kurdistan oil market, a conglomerate today valued at about $1.8 billion—almost all of the value accruing from the rights to their Kurdistan holdings. Some of the firms can be traced back to Al-Qabandi, GIBCA, and the Al-Qassimis. Not only were the Al-Qassimis willing to spend huge amounts of capital to invest in oil operations, but they were also willing to spend lots of money on the Kurdish government.

Wempen, however, was incensed about being dropped. He sued the Kozels in a British court, claiming damages of $1.6 billion. He insisted that Excalibur, although not a party to the Shaikan contract, was entitled to a share of the deal. The heart of the dispute concerned whether the Kozels had entered into a binding partnership with Wempen.

Todd Kozel never disputed that Wempen was the person who first alerted his then-small exploration company to the fact that there were huge opportunities in Kurdistan. What Kozel maintained, however, and what the British court ultimately decided, was that Wempen was a promoter, not an oil man, and he was "not within a country mile" of securing the funds that he promised. Though Wempen and Kozel flirted with a partnership, Kozel understandably ditched Wempen after Hawrami warned him that Wempen's participation would kill Texas Keystone's deal.

Indeed, judge Elizabeth Gloster pulled no punches in her verdict that Excalibur was more or less a shell company. "There was no evidence before me showing that Excalibur had ever

72   participated in any project, or that it possessed the technical
      know-how, capability, or capital required to invest or partici-
      pate in an oil exploration and production venture," Gloster said.

      It did not matter that the Kozels had little success in Gulf
      explorations. Al-Qabandi and Al-Qassimi were far less inter-
      ested in American companies' ability to find and produce oil
      than in finding wheelers and dealers. They opened the way for
      operators like Wempen and Excalibur to try to cash in on the
      Kurdistan oil bonanza. New companies materialized overnight,
      many no more than shells or vehicles through which cash flowed
      to local partners. The majority of transactions were private and
      had no need to report earnings. There was no transparency in the
      investment process because the Kurdish government awarded
      contracts as it saw fit. There was no formal bidding process. No
      one knew what was going on inside Iraqi Kurdistan's growing oil
      sector because little information was disclosed to the public.

      Excalibur Ventures LLC v Texas Keystone Inc and Others,
      however, was a marathon fifty-seven-day hearing, one of the
      longest cases heard by the Commercial Court in the UK. It spun
      off a great raft of documents, and the case showed just how eager
      American oil companies were, and what lengths some adven-
      turers went to, to try to cash in on the chaos that ensued when
      the Kurdish government flung its oil doors open to Western
      wildcatters.

      The system itself was built on small companies eager to
      cash in on the potential of a strengthening Kurdish government
      and a budding oil sector. The Kurds wanted to offload the work
      of exploration on companies that they didn't need in the long

run, and they needed to build the reputation of Kurdistan as a region that people were interested in, to lure larger operations like Gulf Keystone. Early prospectors like Wempen were simply muscled out in favor of bigger players.

In the end, the British Appeals Court ordered Wempen and a number of parties that had spent millions helping to finance Wempen's lawsuit to pay Texas Keystone's legal fees, estimated in some court documents at as much as 30 million pounds.

These days, Wempen heads a company called Northern Resource, formed in 2011, which claims to develop energy and infrastructure projects across the globe, although it is not clear exactly what the company does. In 2012 he founded the non-profit U.S.–Kurdistan Business Council, based in Washington. "Kurdistan has embraced American business, and I believe the U.S. should promote investment and engagement with Erbil," Wempen said in a statement for the council. "USKBC founders, including Excalibur, are pleased to have assisted in the Kurdistan Region's development, and we look forward to continue supporting the region."

Game Changer

ExxonMobil is the largest non-state oil company on the planet, with about $240 billion in annual revenues. It has a $4 billion cash hoard on its books and another $22 billion in operating cash flow. Its oil and gas operations span more than fifty countries around the world. If the Kurdish government was interested in luring brand-name U.S. companies, in 2011 they hooked the biggest fish of all.

Foreign companies like China National Petroleum Corporation, Russia's Lukoil, and British Petroleum had signed oil agreements with Saddam in the 1990s, though it took them years to start development. Foreign firms were not particularly welcomed in Iraq's nationalized oil fields under Saddam, but American corporations like ExxonMobil were even more unwelcome.

Everything changed for ExxonMobil when the bombs started falling on Baghdad in March 2003, for all that the Bush

administration claimed that Iraq would be allowed to control
its own oil fields. From the beginning ExxonMobil, then headed
by Lee Raymond, a longtime friend of U.S. Vice President Dick
Cheney's, was deeply involved in conversations with the U.S.
government's Energy Task Force about natural resource avail-
ability in Iraq, according to financial regulatory enforcement
officers. Soon after the U.S. invasion, the transitional and even-
tual governments of Baghdad did approach international energy
giants. Few of the giants were interested, as Iraq's oil infrastructure was notoriously outdated and wrecked after years
of nationalization and deterioration under Saddam. Raymond
urged caution, predicting that it would be a long time before
it would be worthwhile for ExxonMobil to risk business with
Baghdad, especially with the security and political uncertainty
posed by the war.

The Iraqi government might allow wildcatters to prospect
and explore its fields to get an idea of how much oil was really
underneath, but it wasn't until 2009 that Baghdad was ready
to put up its southern oil fields for bidding, and ExxonMobil
and a partner quickly picked up the rights to the West Qurna-1
field near Basra. Exxon signed a $50 billion technical services
agreement with the Ministry of Oil in Baghdad to redevelop and
rehabilitate the field. Though the terms were less than ideal,
since ExxonMobil was in effect working for the Ministry of Oil,
the field was then considered the most sought after of the nine
available in the country, with verified reserves of 15 billion barrels. (It would take another seven years for ExxonMobil to raise
production from 270,000 barrels a day to 470,000 barrels a day

in 2017. It then sold off parts of the contract, bringing in other international partners.)

Political stability was still elusive in 2011. ExxonMobil, then headed by Rex Tillerson, turned to Ali Khedery, a senior adviser to three U.S. generals and a special assistant to five U.S. ambassadors, to look for other ways into Iraq with better terms— production-sharing agreements instead of technical services agreements. Khedery, who drafted and implemented ExxonMobil's Iraq strategy, argued that with the chaos in Baghdad and elsewhere caused by the U.S. invasion, Kurdistan—where Ashti Hawrami's PSAs were the norm—would be a more profitable and predictable place to do business.

There was a sticking point, however. Erbil and Baghdad, with their on-again, off-again efforts to coordinate Kurdish oil development, had reached an impasse; Baghdad warned companies about cutting deals directly with the Kurds. The U.S. was trying to break the impasse, in part by trying to forge a strong relationship with Nouri al-Maliki, then Prime Minister of Iraq, and his Shia-dominated government. Khedery was no fan of al-Maliki. He thought al-Maliki was a polarizing figure who would deepen the divisions in the country, causing violence and negatively impacting U.S. corporations operating in the country. "I was urging the vice president of the United States and the White House senior staff to withdraw their support for Maliki," Khedery later wrote in the *Washington Post*. "I had come to realize that if he remained in office, he would create a divisive, despotic, and sectarian government." He eventually resigned from the Obama administration in protest.

By January 2011, Khedery was working for ExxonMobil, putting together a plan to reach out to Kurdish officials to negotiate a deal. ExxonMobil's executives spoke to Ashti Hawrami and Masoud Barzani in a series of meetings in Erbil, London, and Dubai. Soon after, ExxonMobil signed exploration agreements with the Kurdish government to develop six oil blocks in the northern part of the region. In the months leading up to the actual signing, Exxon executives informed the State Department and people in the cabinet about the company's plans. U.S. officials, including the ambassador to Iraq, James Jeffrey, were forced to manage the fallout: They gave ExxonMobil an earful about Baghdad's anger. "As ambassador, my goal was to advance the U.S. commercial presence in all of Iraq, especially in strategic oil sector," Jeffrey told me. "Exxon was an important American player, and I worked to ensure good relations between Exxon—and other American companies—and Iraqi and Iraqi Kurdish authorities." But Baghdad was so furious that it threatened to end the company's contract in West Qurna.

Some of the six ExxonMobil blocks lie in territory that continues to be disputed between Baghdad and Erbil. This dispute, indeed, goes to the larger question of exactly where Kurdistan's formal boundaries can be drawn. The ExxonMobil blocks lay in land, defined by Article 140 of the Iraqi Constitution, on which Saddam Hussein had expelled the Kurds in the course of his program to increase Arab population.

The flare-up with Baghdad calmed down by 2013, in part soothed by ExxonMobil bringing aboard as a special adviser none other than Jeffrey. The company also hired former Secretary of

78   State Condoleezza Rice as well as the person who had replaced
her as National Security Advisor, Stephen Hadley. (With former
Defense Secretary Robert Gates, they make up the consulting
firm RiceHadleyGates.) Former ambassador to Iraq Ryan Crocker
also ended up working for ExxonMobil. The corporation now
faced few roadblocks in the Kurdistan projects.

As big a win as Basra and Kurdistan were to ExxonMobil, the
agreements connected the oil giant to even larger deals. One
of the blocks ExxonMobil tapped into was the Al Qush, known
by oil workers as simply "Qush." Komet, a small subsidiary of
Moldova's ASCOM, had held the license to Al Qush before the
Kurdish government withdrew it for lack of development. But
regulatory enforcement officers said ExxonMobil was the corporation that actually funded Komet's operations in Al Qush,
and what it really wanted to know from Komet was whether Al
Qush could lead it to Shaikan, the massive oil discovery that
the Kozel brothers' Gulf Keystone signed on to in 2007, which
sat directly east. Some oil experts, including seismic analysts,
believed part of Shaikan ran into Al Qush.

Another crucial block was Bashiqa, located in the
north-central part of the country. Bashiqa proved to be central to the governorate's economic and political relationship
with Turkey. Since the presidency of Bill Clinton, ExxonMobil
had been lobbying for stronger relationships with Turkey due
to its strategic location as a shipping hub for Middle Eastern
oil. Clinton didn't make relations with Turkey a priority, but
George W. Bush did. The Kurdish and Turkish governments had

been in negotiations to form partnerships on energy deals since
2012. So when ExxonMobil was seeking a partner for Bashiqa,
it tapped Turkey's state-owned Turkish Energy Co., which was
created from scratch in Kurdistan on behalf of Turkey.

While TEC became a minority partner in ExxonMobil's
exploration blocks, the Turkish government acquired an addi-
tional stake in keeping Kurdish oil flowing via the Iraq–Turkey
Ceyhan pipeline. The Kirkuk–Ceyhan pipeline was constructed
in 1974, and it transported oil from Kirkuk to the Turkish port in
Ceyhan, but it was controlled by Baghdad. For years, the Kurds
exported their oil using trucks. In 2012, Turkey and the Kurdish
government began negotiations that would lead to the construction of one new gas and two new oil pipelines from Kurdistan to
Turkey, bypassing Baghdad. The deal even included terms that
allowed Turkey to have a stake in Kurdish oil blocks. The new
Kurdish pipeline was to connect to the Kirkuk–Ceyhan line
just before the Turkish border. Ashti Hawrami said at the time
that the first pipeline would increase the region's total production capacity to one million barrels a day by 2016 and two million barrels per day by 2019. Eventually, the Kurds announced
the line would raise the capacity to three million barrels a day.
(Although the KRG was exporting no more than 600,000 barrels per day as of late 2017.)

It looked as if the new KRG–Turkey pipeline might never be
finished. It faced construction cost overruns, and the Turkish
government had to step in. By 2013, the pipeline was complete:
The first shipments of Kurdistan crude flowed into Turkish
refineries in Ceyhan in the first quarter of 2014. It was reported

80 at the time that the government of Turkey received 5 percent of the total amount of oil that was sold and pumped along the line, through transport and custom duties. But since payments for Kurdistan's oil were deposited in an escrow account opened by the Kurdish government in Halkbank, a Turkish state bank—despite Baghdad's demands that a bank account in the U.S. be used instead—the financial details of the deal were hard to come by, and it was unclear who had control over the funds in the bank. In September 2015, the Kurdish press reported that the KRG's finance minister actually went to Halkbank in Turkey to transfer funds out of the account, but there was actually no money in it.

Baghdad was irate over all of this. Al-Maliki even asked President Obama to step in and force ExxonMobil to halt activities in the Kurdish region, though Obama touted the "one Iraq" policy, and his mind was on committing to his U.S. troop withdrawal. ExxonMobil eventually relinquished its interests in three of its Kurdistan blocks, the Qara Hanjeer, Arbat East and Betwata blocks, in 2016. Some KRG officials said the company pulled out from the blocks because of decreasing production. Hawrami had a different view. "Some companies didn't meet contractual deadlines and according to the contract had to relinquish their areas," he said in a statement at the time of the announcement.

In 2015, Atheel al-Nujaifi, then the governor of Nineveh, even invited Turkey to deploy five hundred troops to protect the Bashiqa block from ISIS, whose presence was beginning to drive Western energy companies from the region. Turkish

troops used the area to train local fighters who acted as a *de facto*
backup security force for ExxonMobil, and who would later join
in the battle to recapture Mosul from ISIS. In October 2016, an
Iraqi court issued an arrest warrant for al-Nujaifi for allowing
Turkish troops into Bashiqa.

Al-Nujaifi was the man whose blessing ExxonMobil needed
to begin exploration and drilling in the disputed Nineveh Governorate. Al-Nujaifi and his brother, Osama (the Speaker of the
Iraqi legislature at the time), were two of the fiercest political
opponents of Prime Minister al-Maliki. "We must be part of
this contract," he said. "I believe that we enjoy the same power
and authority as the government of the Kurdistan region, since
the Constitution does not differentiate between governorates and regions." Al-Nujaifi did indeed meet with ExxonMobil
about the possibility of joining the contract, and according to
financial regulatory enforcement officers, ExxonMobil cut him
and his family in, though the details of that deal remain unclear.

ExxonMobil was undoubtedly a game changer, as the oil
corporations TAQA, Total, Chevron, and Gazprom all eventually followed in its footsteps and signed oil agreements with
the Kurdish government. By 2013 close to forty companies held
contracts, giving the Kurdish government a significant amount
of financial strength, technical expertise, and international
political backing in its confrontation with Baghdad, further
broadening the rift.

Revolving Door

Oil is a fraught business requiring fixers, political connections, and the ability to navigate and abide ceaseless palace intrigue. Production-sharing agreements are negotiated behind closed doors, without a formal bidding process. Kurdish officials refrained from detailing exactly what they were up to, and once they struck a deal, U.S. oil executives never discussed the terms even with their best friends in the oil patch: The Kurds would see that as bad form, since it could alert Baghdad to deals it considered illegal. But according to American financial regulatory officials who were probing the Kurdish operations of U.S. oil companies under the Foreign Corrupt Practices Act, there was one institution dedicated to helping American companies, small and large, navigate the region and understand the complicated politics—the U.S. government.

Peter Galbraith, a former U.S. diplomat and staff member of the Senate Foreign Relations Committee, was tasked in 2003 with helping to draft the new Iraqi constitution that would allow the Kurds to control future oil development. At the same time, he was an advisor to the Norwegian oil company DNO, negotiating deals between that company and the Kurdish government.

The story behind Galbraith's relationship with DNO began with the relationship between the Kurdish government and a company called Pinemont. The Kurdish government had hired Pinemont to develop the region's energy potential, and since Pinemont was especially familiar with the Norwegian market, it reached out to Norsk Hydro, a Norwegian aluminum and renewable energy company, to sign a deal with the KRG. Behind closed doors, Hydro hired a "Norwegian businessman" and a "foreign politician" to help negotiate the contract with the Kurdish government, though senior Hydro executives questioned whether that was transparent enough. When finally Hydro concluded that it was not, the company terminated its development agreement. Hydro did, however, pay the "foreign politician" hundreds of thousands of dollars for his work.

The "Norwegian businessman" was a ship owner named Endre Rosjo who eventually became the chairman and director of Pinemont, and the "foreign politician" was none other than Galbraith, who also worked for Pinemont. When Pinemont was asked to find another Norwegian company for development and exploration in Iraqi Kurdistan, the oil firm DNO took over the Hydro contract—and it included a royalty to Galbraith because he helped negotiate the deal, according to interviews with financial regulatory enforcement officers.

84   Simultaneously, Galbraith formed a company called Por-
cupine that signed a deal with DNO for consultancy services.
Galbraith worked for DNO to negotiate an oil contract for the
Tawke field in Kurdistan, which the company signed onto in
2004. Galbraith told the *New York Times* later that he had held
an "ongoing business relationship" through 2005, even after
DNO signed the contract, despite the fact that he was helping
to negotiate the terms of the Iraqi constitution. Rosjo told the
newspaper that in addition to what he and Galbraith made for
their consultancy work, they also garnered rights of 5 percent
each in the Tawke field. A Yemeni investor ended up taking over
Rosjo's share, and he and Galbraith later took part in an arbitration in London in which they demanded DNO pay them $525
million for their share of Tawke. A British court awarded them
between $55 and $75 million.

     Galbraith eventually admitted he had financial interests
in Kurdish oil dealings at the same time that he was involved in
crafting the Iraqi constitution. But he told the *Boston Globe* in
2009 that he saw no conflict of interest because he was working
as a private citizen at the time. "The business interest, including
my investment into Kurdistan, was consistent with my political
views," he told the newspaper. "These were all things that I was
promoting, and in fact, have brought considerable benefit to the
people of Kurdistan, the Kurdistan oil industry, and also to shareholders." Galbraith would be far from the last American to benefit from their political association with the Kurdish leadership.

     Richard Perle was chairman of the Defense Policy Board
Advisory Committee from 2001 to 2003 under George W. Bush.

According to the *New Yorker* and the *Wall Street Journal*, at the
same time Perle was seeking to sign a contract with a Turkish
firm for the mega-field known as the Khurmala Dome. The
press stories forced Perle to resign as chairman of the advisory
committee.

General Jay Garner had been the first director of the Office
for Reconstruction and Humanitarian Assistance for Iraq—the
office in charge of rebuilding the country after the invasion. In
2008, he joined the board of directors of a Canadian oil exploration company that won a contract in Kurdistan the same year.

And, of course, there was former Iraqi ambassador James
Jeffrey, hired by ExxonMobil to smooth over its Kurdistan
business in 2013. These are just a small sample of those who
walked through government doors right into the lobby of energy
corporations.

American oil companies in turn richly benefited from such
access. Hunt Oil's dealings were perhaps the most controversial. CEO Ray Hunt was an important George W. Bush campaign
donor who had even served on the administration's Foreign
Intelligence Advisory Board. In 2007, Hunt Oil invested in a
block in Iraqi Kurdistan, even though it may have been tech-
nically illegal to do so without permission from the central
government in Baghdad. Baghdad, as it had done with Exxon-
Mobil's Kurdistan investment, complained that the Hunt Oil
contract jeopardized the efforts of the Iraqi parliament to come
to an agreement on national oil legislation.

But unlike ExxonMobil, who only informed the U.S. government after a deal was signed, Bush administration officials

86   knew of the transaction in Kurdistan, and some even supported it, an investigation later found. "There was no commu-
nication to me or in my presence made by any of the nine State
Department officials with whom I met prior to 8 September
that Hunt should not pursue our course of action leading to a
contract," David McDonald, the general manager for Hunt Oil,
said. "In fact there was ample opportunity to do so, but it did not
happen." A Commerce Department official even alerted Hunt
Oil as to which other companies were also seeking oil exploration contracts.

Five days after the company signed a contract with the
Kurdish government, the State Department reached out to
Hunt officials and suggested another business opportunity to
develop a liquefied natural gas refinery in southern Iraq. "This
is really good for us," a Hunt official wrote as he forwarded the
email to Ray Hunt. "I find it a huge compliment that he is 'tip-
ping' us off about this. He certainly doesn't have to . . . this is a
lucky break."

When news of the deal broke, the Bush administration
claimed it had no idea that Hunt was planning the investment.
When President Bush was asked about the contract he said: "I
knew nothing about the deal. I need to know exactly how it happened. To the extent that it does undermine the ability for the
government to come up with an oil revenue sharing plan that
unifies the country, obviously if it undermines it I'm concerned."

The scandal led Henry Waxman, chairman of the House
Committee on Government Oversight and Reform, to open a
high-profile investigation into the matter in 2008, and evidence

he was given led him to call Bush's claim of ignorance into question. "The documents that the Committee has received tell a different story about the role of Administration officials," Waxman later wrote to Secretary of State Condoleezza Rice. "Ray Hunt, the head of Hunt Oil, personally informed advisors to President Bush of meetings he and other Hunt Oil officials planned with representatives of the Kurdish government. Other Hunt Oil officials kept State Department officials informed about the company's intentions." When Waxman closed the proceedings and gave his report, nothing much came of it. Hunt Oil still operates in Kurdistan today.

The revolving door was not a pattern limited to American officials and companies. Nadhim Zahawi, a British Conservative Party politician who is a Member of Parliament for Stratford-on-Avon, was nine years old when he and his parents fled Iraq to the United Kingdom, as the crackdown on the Kurdish people intensified under Saddam Hussein. In the last five years, Zahawi has visited the region several times, appearing on panels with minister Ashti Hawrami. Each time the Kurdish government paid for Zahawi's flights and accommodations. After serving as an adviser for another oil company, Afren, which went bankrupt, Zahawi was appointed chief strategy officer for the Kozel brothers' Gulf Keystone in 2015. Members of Parliament by law have to register their interests within twenty-eight days, but Zahawi did not disclose his position in the company until after that time period. He earned more than $350,000 a year from Gulf Keystone, not including bonuses, for working seven hours a month, in addition to his parliamentary salary. Members of

88   the Kurdish government, particularly those involved in over-seeing the oil and gas sectors, said in interviews in August 2016 that Zahawi was a household name in the KRG, whose influence in the Ministry of Natural Resources paralleled that of Todd Kozel himself. According to a report by *The Guardian*, when Kozel considered selling Gulf Keystone amid serious financial troubles in 2015, Zahawi was set to earn nearly $2 million from the potential sale.

Strange Cargo

On a hot day in September 2007, workers at the Jebel Ali port in Dubai readied to load five oversized packages onto a large cargo ship. For these men, it was a normal day at the port, one of the world's busiest set in one of the world's largest manmade harbors. Trucks rumbled down wide corridors, trundling past tens of thousands of shipping containers. Massive yellow cranes hovered above three-hundred-foot cargo ships. Three of the containers, loaded aboard a Maersk-badged vessel, would later catch the eye of investigators looking into corruption in Kurdistan's oil and gas sector.

The five containers held brand new sport utility vehicles worth more than $1.2 million. Bound for the Turkish port of Mersin, they were eventually destined for recipients in Iraqi Kurdistan. The sender and coordinator of the shipment, according to documents provided by an international regulatory enforcement officer, was Crescent Petroleum. Crescent,

90 one of the Middle East's oldest, largest, and most profitable
energy consortiums, enjoyed major operations with the Kurdistan Regional Government. The vehicles were headed to Crescent's Iraq office to be distributed to Hawrami and his team,
according to Maersk shipping documents and internal Kurdish
government emails.

The emails reveal detailed exchanges between Hamid
Jafar, a Crescent director, and Sarbaz Hawrami, Ashti Hawrami's uncle, who at the time was also Prime Minister Nechirvan
Barzani's secretary. Copied on the email were Badr Jafar, Majid
Jafar, and Ravi Kumar, all members of the company's executive
committee, and Salem Rozoky, the branch manager of Crescent's Erbil office.

> Dear Kak Sarbaz:
>
> The urgent email below about arrival of the SUV vehicles
> (inside containers) at Mersin on the 3rd October is self-
> explanatory. I hope that you have made arrangements for
> your representative to clear and take delivery at Mersin,
> and then onward transportation to Erbil. I have asked Kak
> Salem Razoky, General Manager of Crescent in Erbil, to
> discreetly liaise with you to ensure full coordination.
>
> Best Regards, Hamid

Ravi Kumar wrote back in response to Hamid's email, clar-
ifying the details of the shipment with Sarbaz Hawrami. "To
facilitate a smooth handover of the cars we have now obtained

detailed instructions from Gulftainer, our transportation company, for the clearance and transportation of the cargo," Kumar wrote on October 1, 2007. Kumar went on to lay out in fine detail how the cars would reach Erbil, mentioning that the Kurdish government needed to hire its own trucking company to bring the containers into Iraq and that it had to make direct arrangements for the customs clearance, otherwise customs could levy $16,000 in fines on the shipment.

U.S. and UK investigators, who got these emails as part of a wide-ranging probe of Kurdistan oil contracts, say what was going on here was Hawrami making companies pay to play. The "bonus" payments stipulated in the production-sharing agreements that Hawrami required were often manifested in bribes like these SUVs. Mandated for every contract were "signature bonuses," money due upon signing of a contract. And frequently asked for were "capacity-building bonuses" based on government approval of an oil company's request to expand its production. There were also "local building bonuses"—money ostensibly to finance government infrastructure projects. Companies were also often required to contribute training funds and make contributions to environmental funds. These types of funds are normal on natural resource contracts implemented throughout the world, but what made the KRG bonuses different was a severe lack of transparency. The more money that came into the Ministry of Natural Resources, the harder it was to track, investigators said. Officials in the KRG's own finance ministry admitted to me that they didn't know exactly what happened with the funds.

92   All of these allegations need to be understood against the backdrop of what had been going on in the Ministry of Natural Resources. In Erbil, plans were afoot by the Kurdistan Parliament to solidify the natural resource sector under Hawrami, who was scrambling to get a raft of previously signed contracts aligned with terms laid out in a draft Kurdish hydrocarbon law, which would allow international oil companies to contract with the regional government without gaining permission from Baghdad first. Officially known as the Kurdistan Oil and Gas Law, it would win parliamentary approval on August 6, 2007 and go into effect on August 9, just a few weeks before the SUV shipment would arrive.

Companies like Crescent had a lot riding on the new law and, according to investigators, needed to keep the Kurdish political players happy. Hawrami had already garnered a reputation for arbitrarily rewriting major contracts, and Crescent wanted to avoid that. Its wholly owned subsidiary, Dana Gas, had scored big by winning a contract to develop the Khor Mor and Chamchamal fields in the southeast sector of Iraqi Kurdistan. According to emails, the SUVs crossed the Turkish-Iraq border without a hitch and arrived in Erbil on October 3. Dana's contracts not only survived intact, but the company was allowed to expand its gas operations, doubling output to 300 million cubic feet of gas per day by early 2009. Dana's estimate for total investment in the project rose to $650 million from the $400 million the year before.

However, things between the Kurdish government and Dana would later turn sour. Dana and Crescent filed an arbitration case against the Kurdish government before the London Court of International Arbitration in 2013, arguing that the KRG had arbitrarily slowed or blocked expansion of its operations, and the court ruled in February 2017 in favor of the companies. The KRG was ordered to pay the claimants about $121 million they said they were owed for natural gas extractions between 2015 and 2016. Contracts also show that Westernzagros (whose case is described in Chapter Three) had paid the Kurdish government $40 million in "capacity building bonuses." It's unclear what capacity was built by the funds.

U.S. and UK investigators weren't alone in investigating kickback allegations. In March of 2015, South Korea's National Assembly opened an official inquiry into state-run Korea National Oil Corp's $31.4 million "signature bonus" payments in late 2008 to the Kurdish government. KNOC won concessions to explore and develop the Bazian block near the Kurdish-Iranian border, estimated to hold as much as 1.2 billion barrels of oil.

Chun Soon-ok, a congresswoman of the opposition New Politics Alliance for Democracy, told reporters that a preliminary investigation showed the "signature bonus" money "disappeared" after wire transfers were processed by the banking giant HSBC. Chun said the cash was likely divided between Korean political operatives and people in the Kurdish government, specifically citing Hawrami, who had designated HSBC's London Canary Wharf branch to make the transfer. According to the *Korea Times*, KNOC further wired $100 million in August 2012 and another $10 million in January 2014, ostensibly earmarked

94 to help in the construction of hospitals and other facilities in Kurdistan. There is no indication that those funds were used that way.

According to interviews with investigators and State Department cables, corruption is pervasive throughout the Kurdistan bureaucracy. They say that salaries are paid to fake employees, and that there are massive counterfeiting schemes. "Even Kurdish officials acknowledge that most ministries could operate as effectively with one-third the staff," Michael Rubin, a former Pentagon official, has written. "Less visible but just as endemic is the inflation of government ledgers with ghost employees. Simply put, the government claims extra employees whose salaries officials pocket. There are many variations on this scheme. Some employees might be fictional, but that is dangerous and could lead to exposure. In most cases, ministers, commanders, and directors-general inflate their employee rolls with friends and family. The government disburses the full salary, but the director might give only half to the fake employee, keeping a healthy cut for himself. As Kurdish salaries grow, it must be nice to collect several of them." Arrests and prosecutions remain rare.

Even some of Kurdistan's most public fighters against government corruption have been pulled into the mire. Sherko Jawdat, a member of the Kurdistan Islamic Union Party and chairman of the Parliament Energy Committee, earned a reputation for speaking out for transparency. "There are opportunities now for renegotiation [of oil contracts] but it's not easy because of corruption and we have big battles ahead," he told a Kurdish

media outlet in 2014. "Just as the Peshmerga are fighting Daesh
on the borders, we are fighting corruption. We have the same
role—to create a better Kurdistan."

Later revelations, published by Kurdish journalists, were
especially shocking. Jawdat, it turned out, was privy to the
Kurdish government's defense strategy in the Dana case, since
he regularly sat in on secret meetings. In fact, Jawdat had for
months been passing on the relevant content of those meetings
to a Dana senior executive. "I had a phone call with Dr. Sherko
Jawdat today," Shakir, the country manager at Dana Gas, wrote
in an email to company senior management in 2014. "He told
me that Dana Gas arbitration was discussed for thirty minutes.
I will meet Sherko to know the whole story and also to brief him
before he meets AH"—Ashti Hawrami.

In one email, Jawdat reaches out to an officer of the company and asks him to consider employing his family member.
"Dear Brother Kak Shakir," Jawdat writes. "Mr. Qane Ahmed
Sulaiman has a BA in English and has been an HR manager
for several major companies. He is a professional and reliable
person and is interested in working for Dana Gas. I am seeking
your kind support in helping him get a post in your company.
Please pass my regards to your father." Shakir writes the CEO of
the company: "Dear Kak Majid, I have received attached request
from Dr. Sherko. I suggest you . . . find the candidate a space as
per his qualifications and experience."

The revelations shattered Jawdat's reputation. In June of
2016, the Ministry of Natural Resources sued him for alleging
that the ministry had stolen oil revenue that rightfully belonged

96   to the people of Kurdistan. For a while, Jawdat's collusion with Dana and the resulting lawsuit sent him into seclusion. In recent months, though, Jawdat has been back on television, talking about oil. He has most recently spoken about the Kurdish referendum, claiming any vote without an active parliament is illegal.

The Sufferings of Corruption

Almost ten years ago, Goran Mustafa crashed his car on one of the main roadways in Erbil, shattering his shinbone. Since then, he has worked almost every day to rebuild the muscles in his calf. He still can't walk without a small limp, though he plays soccer weekly and exercises at his local gym.

"I sit there and I move my leg and somehow the doctor thinks I am disabled. He says he can write a paper that says I am disabled so I can earn money from the government," Mustafa tells me.

Mustafa receives disability benefits, but he also works as an advisor to the Kurdish finance ministry and to the Department of Coordination and Follow Up, proposing policies for financial reform. Instances like Mustafa's explain how the public service sector in Iraqi Kurdistan has grown from one that was manageable even under a declining economy to a size so impossibly big that it seems untenable even to the smartest economists.

The bureaucracy led the cabinet to cut high-ranking officials' salaries by a whopping 75 percent in 2016, while payroll
for lower-level employees went down by as much as 20 percent.
There are thousands of people on the government payroll that
shouldn't be on it, Mustafa says, but it is impossible to iden-
tify them without extensive audits. "It takes a long time to go
through all the lists of people and call them to ensure they are
who they say they are," he explains.

Kurdish officials, however, put much of the blame for the
region's crumbling economy not on bloated payrolls or on the
lack of accountability and transparency, but on other matters
seemingly out of their control. They blame the influx of Syrian
refugees and internally displaced Iraqis fleeing from ISIS, or the
government in Baghdad, as the oil export feud between Erbil
and Baghdad drags on.

The Kurds still adamantly maintain they have a right to
not only develop their own natural resource sector, but also to
manage their own oil finances without routing them through
the central government, whereas Baghdad maintains that all oil
revenues must flow through the capital for later distribution. A
draft 2007 national hydrocarbon law that might have resolved
the impasse never made it to a vote, because the Iraqi Parliament couldn't come to an agreement on the terms. That same
year, the Kurdish government passed its own oil and gas law,
which didn't help matters.

Many Kurds are so fiercely loyal to the notion of Kurdish
independence that government corruption and fraud are for-
gotten amid resentment toward Baghdad. Part of turning this

blind eye to corruption is that for a while it didn't seem to matter economically. The region's GDP grew by almost 7 percent between 2007 and 2010, and it wasn't only the oil and gas sector that was booming: Foreign direct investments in real estate and tourism were rising. As late as the summer of 2014, when the Kurdish military took over oil wells at Bai Hassan and others in Kirkuk, the oil markets were in a very different place. Oil was selling at about $103 a barrel, and the Kurds had a window to sell on the international market through Turkey. Iraqi Kurdistan seemed to have achieved a rather remarkable thing, all things considered.

According to a November 2015 report by Reuters, one of the KRG's secret assets was a Pakistani oil trader named Murtaza Lakhani. "He knew exactly who would and who wouldn't deal with us," Ashti Hawrami told the news agency. "He opened the doors to us and identified willing shipping companies to work with us." At around the same time Lakhani told the *Financial Times* that he had helped the Kurdish government arrange pipeline oil sales and liaised with international traders to bypass Baghdad's attempts to block Kurdish actions. "I get my hands dirty," Lakhani told the newspaper. "I've been in the Iraq region for sixteen years and in Kurdistan long before anyone else. I'm keeping the KRG's oil sales business operationally running."

When the dispute with Baghdad intensified, not only did the export spigot dry up, but Baghdad held up Kurdish gains as proof that the central government was being cheated of its rightful share of the oil money. It stopped sending the KRG the required 17 percent of its federal budget as mandated by the Iraqi constitution.

When the price of oil dropped to as low as $24 a barrel at one point in 2016, Kurdistan's economic growth stalled and unemployment rose, according to the finance ministry in Erbil. Tens of thousands of civil servants were not paid for months, forcing many of them to leave or find second jobs. Meanwhile, Iraqi Kurdistan's top families and loyal government officials continued to enrich themselves.

The dichotomy between those who have capitalized on Iraqi Kurdistan's oil and those who haven't can even be seen in the physical layout of Erbil. Near the international airport, fifty-story apartment buildings, adorned with crystal chandeliers, tower over the garbage collectors who pick up the trash in the luxury complexes each day. The apartments house international oil traders and contractors, as well as government employees linked to the oil market. Next to the apartment complex sits the Divan Hotel, a lavish building that provides lodging for international traders and businessmen. Rooms run to more than $300 a night. Behind the building lies a makeshift refugee camp that houses thirty Yazidi refugee families who fled the predations of ISIS; they are hungry, and say government and charitable food assistance is inconsistent.

Next to the ancient citadel downtown, gold merchants sit slumped over their glass cabinets holding dozens of necklaces, earrings, and bracelets. "It's been slow here for about a year," one merchant says, nervously rearranging the gold jewelry on his felt trays. "Our profits are down about 20 percent."

At his office in the rambling government-run Rizgary Hospital, Dr. Shakhawan Dizayee, the facility's manager, sits in a leather chair in front of his desk. He's dressed in a button-down shirt and quality shoes bought in London. Coming from a wealthy family close to the KDP leadership, he uses what's left of his inheritance to live in Royal City, the lavish apartment complex across from the Divan Hotel, and sends his daughter to a prestigious high school near the border with Iran. She will attend university in London, he says. "You see," he continues, "I come from a rich family. So, for me, this crisis doesn't really affect me. If I could go back and change things, though, I wouldn't be a doctor here. But I am too old to start a new life now. My daughter is still young. She has a chance at a better future."

But his hospital, Erbil's largest, is suffering, as are its employees and patients. He has just $13,000 per month to spend on maintenance and upkeep, far less than he says he needs. "The other month our elevator broke — the one that goes to the operating floor. And I had no money to fix it." All of Kurdistan depends on his hospital's single CAT scan machine. If it breaks? There's not enough money to replace it, he tells me.

Dizayee oversees 1,700 employees. Most of them work two or three jobs. Sometimes, they don't show up because they make more money in their other professions. "My job here requires that I discipline them, that I yell at them," the doctor says. "I don't feel like I can. I can't blame them for wanting to make money. But at the same time, it makes my job really hard." High-level doctors at Rizgary like Dizayee make just $500 a month.

During better times, they made close to $2,500 a month. Doctors below him in rank make even less—about $200 a month. Thousands of doctors have fled Erbil since 2014 and are now practicing in Europe, Dizayee says. Those who remain often leave their public jobs at 1:00 p.m. and go to their more lucrative private clinics, where they work until about 9:00 p.m. Others work as taxi drivers or policemen.

Deteriorating conditions at Rizgary mimic the city as a whole. In some wings, walls have gaping holes. The emergency room on the first floor is overflowing with patients. Dozens sit in the hallway, eating bits of bread and dates, waiting for a turn to talk to a doctor or nurse. Because of the lack of available specialists, the emergency room here acts as a filter for all non-surgical patients. It also has one of the only blood laboratories in the city.

By the early afternoon, Rizgary's operating floor is empty and silent. All the doctors have left for their other jobs. "Sometimes I think I should just move to London and stay there," says Dizayee dejectedly. "It has more opportunity. But my extended family needs me here. They need my support." A pile of dirty scrubs lies on the floor. Bloodied clogs line the hallway outside the operating theater.

The ISIS Oil Grab

On June 10, 2014, the northern Iraqi city of Mosul was a mess.

Camouflage uniforms, helmets, and white underwear littered the ground, abandoned by the Iraqi military. Soldiers had fled en masse when machine-gun-toting ISIS militants stormed Mosul in Toyota pickup trucks.

It wasn't simply fear that caused the Iraqis to abandon their posts. They were already a demoralized bunch, most of them Sunni Muslims who felt little allegiance to then Prime Minister Nouri al-Maliki, a Shiite whom they both mistrusted and resented. They had been sidelined from promotions under his regime, and they hadn't been paid in months.

The shock of the ISIS blitzkrieg changed the dynamics in Iraq overnight. The extremist group captured vast swathes of land along the highway that led straight to Baghdad, and in the minds of many ordinary Iraqis, they seemed unstoppable. The insurgency that had first gained ground in the

Sunni stronghold of Fallujah during the early days of the U.S. occupation had grown into a group that now controlled one of Iraq's largest cities, with ISIS leader Abu Bakr al-Baghdadi declaring the founding of a new caliphate. ISIS spread like a cancer, overrunning small towns and capturing oil wells, pipelines, and entire oil fields.

The week that ISIS took Mosul, it seized a key government checkpoint, and acquired the ability to transport fighters, weapons, money, and oil internationally. Its stunning success proved a potent recruiting tool in the Sunni-dominated towns in both eastern Syria and western Iraq. ISIS ranks swelled with tens of thousands of fighters. Mosul became its de facto headquarters in Iraq, while Raqqa served as its capital in Syria.

ISIS's reign of terror seemed to emerge suddenly, but the group had actually been systematically building up a base of fighters and weapons. Some were Sunni officers from the Iraqi Army or Ba'athists marginalized by the Shiite-dominated government. Others came from Syria or were fresh recruits. The group carried out forced recruitments. Foreigners in some places were offered $700 a month to train and fight. That kind of money was more than many men could make in an entire year in regular employment. ISIS also recruited among Palestinians in refugee camps in Lebanon and Jordan, as well as radicalizing vulnerable young Muslims in Turkey, the West, and Asia, all the while massacring opponents in the Yarmouk camp in Damascus.

I arrived in Iraqi Kurdistan one day after the fall of Mosul, as I traveled from Erbil to the contested city of Tuz Khurmatu, about fifty miles south of Kirkuk. ISIS was in the process of taking over small villages nearby. At a Kurdish base outside the town, a white truck with a floral print mattress strapped to the top puttered down the road, stopping at an unmanned checkpoint. Inside the truck, a father and his five young daughters held most of their household belongings on their laps. "We are going to Kirkuk and then on to Erbil to try and find housing there," the father says. "Daesh"—referring to ISIS's Arabic acronym, which the group considers derogatory—"is coming, so we are just trying to get away."

Some of the territory north and east of Kirkuk was being patrolled by the Kurdish Peshmerga forces, while other strategic locations were defended by soldiers under Baghdad's Ministry of Defense and the Shiite Popular Mobilization Forces. Coalition forces coordinated air support and intelligence from Erbil with Kurdish Peshmerga officers. The commander of the Peshmerga base walked out to greet me, wearing a camouflage uniform that stretched at the seams, his protruding belly prevented him from buttoning the middle latch. Local lore based on centuries of history has it that the Kurds are warriors and the only ones who can defeat ISIS. The men in this camp, though, seem out of shape and largely untested. They admit later that they hadn't fought since the Kurdish uprising against Saddam and its aftermath in the 1990s.

Inside the camp, a three-building compound and a garage filled with ammunition, men wandered the halls in sandals and shorts. Some cleaned their weapons and inspected the few American-made Humvees in the field, leftovers from the U.S.

military presence. The atmosphere was drowsy. On the compound's roof, a soldier sat in a plastic chair, binoculars slung around his neck. He handed them to me.

"Look," he says in English. "Daesh." As my eyes adjust, I scan left and right and finally see something—the black flag of ISIS. Beneath the flag, men walked about inside a concrete compound, AK-47s slung over their backs.

ISIS had taken over the small compound outside Tuz Khurmatu just the week before. Both the Kurds and ISIS knew the stakes. Whoever held Tuz Khurmatu would have a straight shot to Baghdad, a mere two-hour drive to the south. They would also be in position to commandeer the oilfields of Kirkuk, fifty miles to the north, and access the road leading to Sulaymaniyah, another oil-rich governorate, a hundred-and-fifteen-mile drive northeast.

The Kurdish forces said they felt marginalized by al-Maliki and blamed poor military leadership as part of the reason Mosul fell so quickly. Still, this band of Peshmerga was almost gleeful at the Iraqi army's desertion of Mosul: The Kurds were now closer to controlling the oil fields and the revenue it would bring.

Daquq, midway between Tuz Khurmatu and Kirkuk, is a multi-ethnic river town. The district consists of about 70,000 people and is best known for its ornate mosque and tea plantations. But these days all the talk is about ISIS. On this visit to Iraq in June 2014, Daquq is home to yet another military outpost abandoned by the Iraqi army when ISIS invaded. About six hundred Peshmerga fighters filled the void. Happily for them,

the fleeing Iraqi army also abandoned their armored vehicles,
heavy Katyusha rocket launchers, rocket-propelled grenades,
and machine guns.

"For a long time we have wanted to take back this base.
When we came here, we did not need to fight the military. They
just left because they did not want to fight ISIS," the Kurdish
official from Daquq told me. "ISIS might be able to beat Maliki,
but they can't beat us. Maliki's soldiers fight for money, not for
their country." In reality, however, these men were rusty. Before
the fall of Mosul, many of them were stationed in relatively tran-
quil locations. Some of them had only met up the week prior.

Kurdish military leaders here told me that they relied on
local villagers to inform them of ISIS movements. The officers sent fighters out every six hours to patrol the area. Snipers
manned the rooftops of buildings, watching for intruders. Yet
the Peshmerga said they feared that ISIS could infiltrate the
area unexpectedly, taking advantage of local collaboration. In
some areas nearby, Sunni families had taken up arms in support
of ISIS, the Kurdish fighters said, but it wasn't clear who had
pledged formal allegiance to the militant group. Some Sunni
clans were suspected, and the Kurds tried to negotiate with
their leaders to join the Kurds instead of ISIS. "We will defend
this area until we die," a commander at the base in Kirkuk said.
"We have the soul needed to defend our land. I don't think ISIS
can beat us."

ISIS's strategy was simple: Capture as much oil and land as
possible. They would cut off official exports and sell that oil on
the black market at the inflated prices the violence had created,

often using the Saddam regime's smuggling routes in western Anbar Province to do so. At the height of its successes in 2014 and 2015, the group's largely unmonitored scheme was raking in an estimated $1 million a day, according to a report by the U.S. Treasury Department. Some experts say it could have been twice that. ISIS also made tens of millions of dollars from the ransom demanded from kidnappings, taxing the areas it controlled, and stealing and selling antiquities. ISIS had become, in the words of Richard Cohen, the Treasury's undersecretary for Terrorism and Financial Intelligence, "one of the best-funded terrorist organizations we have ever confronted."

Brigadier General Sarhad Qadir, commanding the police in Kirkuk and its sub districts, said that in the beginning, ISIS had help. Local Kurdish oil workers—middlemen who operated tanker trucks transporting legitimate oil to Turkey and Iran—collaborated with the terrorist group, selling some of that oil to ISIS. ISIS would then sell the oil on the black market, in villages where its own predations had caused shortages and inflated prices, pocketing the steep profits. According to a report written by George Kiourktsoglou and Alec Coutroubis, researchers at the University of Greenwich who study the group's oil business, ISIS sold the bulk of its oil in this way, within the region. It "exported anywhere from 3,000 to 8,000 barrels a day, about 15 percent of its total production, for sale on the high seas in 2014," Kiourktsoglou told me. Qadir said that sometimes ISIS operatives would pay off workers who were guarding the Kirkuk—Ceyhan pipeline's access points to siphon off oil for them. The operators and smugglers responsible for transporting and

selling ISIS's oil would send convoys of as many as thirty trucks
at a time to these extraction sites.

Sometimes the group hired people to truck the oil to Turkey on the international E90 route, which twists and turns its way from the Iraqi-Turkish border west to Lisbon, the Portuguese capital. Once in Turkey, the oil would be refined in the southeastern part of the country before sale at either the port of Ceyhan or Dortyol, which is located directly across the bay. Other times, ISIS passed off the oil to middlemen who mixed it with oil produced by legitimate American and European energy companies for transport to Turkey, according to a senior official in Erbil.

The oil system from Iraqi Kurdistan to eastern Syria is an intricate maze of small lines that lead to the Kirkuk–Ceyhan pipeline, which every major company in the region uses to transport its oil to ports. A network of roads connects various pipeline entry points to oil fields and refineries. Much like an effective money-laundering operation, it was nearly impossible for officials at the end of the pipeline in Turkey to determine illicit batches of oil from those produced by legitimate energy companies.

"Oil is fungible, it is hard to track," former U.S. ambassador to Iraq James Jeffrey said. "Smuggling was happening under our noses in the 1990s, and we tried to stop it. But the smuggling of oil business into Turkey is deeply rooted in infrastructure. It is impossible to shut down without shutting down the entire thing."

Thankfully, by the fall of 2015, ISIS oil sales were severely diminished by U.S. airstrikes on ISIS oil facilities. Eventually, by 2016, ISIS completely lost control of the oil fields. Now, the Iraqi government is trying to finalize plans to refurbish and restart production at the fields ISIS once held.

Although the terrorist group has lost complete control of oil fields, it still attacks oil wells. In October of 2017, local news outlets reported that the group set several different wells on fire west of the city of Kirkuk near the town of Hawija. ISIS frequently set oil wells ablaze throughout the three-year-long battle as a way to avoid coalition airstrikes.

The oil black market in Iraq is still operational but it is unclear how many barrels of oil are being siphoned off per day.

The Guardians of the Treasure

Iraqi Kurdistan's frustration over the oil export impasse with Baghdad is eclipsed by another concern: keeping its vast reserves under Kurdish command and out of the hands of ISIS. Which explains why these days, despite the hard economic times, the government in Erbil, in coordination with local councils, has greatly bolstered spending on military and police.

It is the job of Kirkuk police commander Sarhad Qadir to protect not just wells, but entire oil fields and the pipelines serving them. The military compound where Qadir works is ringed in by concrete walls, and dozens of armed men sit at checkpoints on the main road leading from the highway to the offices inside the compound. The atmosphere inside, however, is surprisingly relaxed. Men stroll around a garden, smoking cigarettes and exchanging jokes. Our meeting with Qadir is postponed for three hours, so we wait in the courtyard and visit with the media team, whose members are putting together video footage of security forces manning the oil fields.

Qadir's office walls are lined with photographs of him with American officials and diplomats who served under the Bush administration, whom Qadir worked with to track down Al-Qaeda members in Kirkuk during the 2003 war. Now, he's doing the same thing with ISIS, but ISIS seems to have far more money than Al-Qaeda had. No terrorist group has ever had access to that much cash.

"The government contracted with the local villages to hire people to protect the oil rigs," Qadir explains. But these contractors often failed in their duties. "With that set up, there were gaps in security that allowed for terrorists to explode pipelines and steal oil." Since then, the Kurds have decided they needed to create a robust counterterrorism force that focuses on infiltrating ISIS cells to stop attacks before they happen. "Every month it feels like dozens of oil employees are getting killed by ISIS attacks," Qadir says. "There's so much infrastructure in this area that ISIS wants, because if you have Kirkuk, you have all of Iraq." Collusion is still a problem, as some oil workers help the terrorist network by transporting stolen oil, or even feed the group information about how to attack the pipelines.

The Kurds have had success cracking down on the oil smuggling that so enriched ISIS. "At the beginning of the conflict, this [smuggling] used to happen a lot," Qadir says. Since the Kurds have regained control of their own security, Qadir's team has been better equipped to deal with the problem. From 2014 to early 2015, Qadir says he arrested dozens of ISIS terrorists who took oil from their wells. These days, arrests are becoming rare, because the Iraqi military, along with American advisors, have pushed ISIS out of oil-rich areas in the region. The terror group is at last on the defensive, remaining active only in its last Iraqi and Syrian bastions.

To see Kurdistan's vast oilfields, you have to drive from Erbil toward Kirkuk, past a poor village with crumbling buildings that have no roofs, on potholed streets that aren't paved, featuring just one restaurant, covered in dust, that serves fish from a nearby river. At an intersection, young children line up to buy colored ice in paper cups from a vendor manning a mobile cooler. Five miles past the village, vast cornfields that feed the villagers give way to an arid landscape of jagged boulders. Gigantic slabs of rocks jut from the ground, looking unnatural, as if some great unseen hand had carved them. As we drive on, ever bigger craters and slabs of stone block our path. We feel like we're driving on Mars.

The barren landscape would seem to match the poverty of the village we've just left behind. But, in fact, once you reach Dibis, a town forty minutes northwest of Kirkuk, you'll have reached some of Kurdistan's richest oilfields. This is the heart of the Kurdish government's cash machine, and the fields are protected by some of the most well-trained and best-equipped soldiers in the region.

Night has fallen, and the soldiers, security guards from the region's oil and gas police armed with AK-47s, jump into the back of an open Jeep. We follow, down a rocky road that then leads up a hill to a ridge high above town, to a breathtaking vantage point. A massive oil field stretches seemingly forever under the black desert sky, shooting orange flames into the air from wells flaring toxins and excess natural gas. When these fields were overrun by ISIS in August 2016, the terror group's operatives blew up part of the pipeline running through town: Oil flowed through the streets of Dibis for days before the rupture could be repaired.

I've come to see the man who knows more about the running battle with ISIS than perhaps anyone in Kurdistan: Commander Kamal Kirkuki, a veteran Peshmerga from the Kurdistan Democratic Party, and a former speaker of Parliament. Kirkuki, who is in his mid-sixties, is a slender man, unassuming in his traditional Kurdish clothing. Kirkuki commands the Peshmerga's elite, front-line troops here, policing Dibis and its surrounding villages—and, as a priority, the oil and gas fields.

As Kirkuki dims the lights, a large projector drops from the ceiling, and he runs through the same presentation he gave to representatives of the U.S. military just minutes earlier. The Peshmerga had received new intelligence from U.S. drone footage of ISIS fighters hiding out in a nearby house. The drone captured footage of a car driving down a dirt road and into a small driveway. "This house is where about twenty soldiers are hiding. They're going into that house now, but they won't come out again."

The projector goes black, and Kirkuki moves to a large wall map, adorned with thumbtacks marking different positions on the battlefield—red for ISIS and blue for the Peshmerga.

As he moves the blue and red tacks to describe a huge battle in 2015, he reveals the secret to his successes against the terrorist group: "Every movement we made was about protecting the oil," Kirkuki says. Our meeting is interrupted when a group of his fighters enter the room, stamping their feet in salute. Unlike the out-of-shape Kurdish soldiers I encountered in Daquq, these men are tall, fit, imposing, and look ready for battle.

"Our job is to protect the oil companies," one of them tells me as he hops from a Jeep to begin a patrol. Flares from a nearby refinery illuminate the night sky.

"Our economy," he says, "depends on it."

No Place Like Home

Inside a shipping container that's become his home, Ahmed Qusai scoops up his son from a mattress on the concrete floor and kisses him on the cheek. Qusai used to be an oil worker in Qayyarah, a once energy-rich town about forty-five miles south of Mosul. He now lives in the Debaga refugee camp outside Erbil. It's hard to find a quiet place in the overcrowded slums, as Qusai rocks the child back and forth to calm his tired cries. Black smoke from oilfield fires cloud the horizon—a reminder of both the life Qusai used to live and a sign of war that's still raging.

In late August of 2016, the Iraqi army and its allies freed Qayyarah from ISIS, calling it a key step in the campaign to retake Mosul. But victory came at a price. ISIS fighters dug in, setting fire to oil wells, pipelines, and a nearby sulfur plant, and destroying the house Qusai had built for his family. Crude from those attacks and counterattacks still ran unchecked through the streets of Qayyarah during my visit there. The town on the banks of the Tigris River once supported a population of about 15,000 people. These days, it's a smoky, sooty disaster area.

Like thousands of men in this camp, Qusai once worked with Western energy companies, helping to produce Kurdistan's most valuable asset. Now, thanks to ISIS's own thirst for oil, Qusai spends his days cleaning his prefabricated shelter and walking the aisles of the camp, home to about 35,000 refugees. Qusai tells me that he's not only angry at ISIS but at his own government. "We weren't happy living there," Qussai says, as he points to images on a flickering TV screen of the ruins of his hometown. "We weren't getting any of the benefits of the oil we were protecting. The government just took the oil and didn't work with the local people."

Qusai and his friends were still guarding the oil fields when ISIS came tearing through in early 2014. He had been trained by representatives of the foreign oil companies that arrived en masse after the toppling of Saddam's regime in 2003, as the West promised to develop the region's potential. As late as 2014, there was still talk of a Kurdish economic "miracle": Exports and growth increased steadily, and members of the Kurdish diaspora—the thousands of Kurds who had fled Saddam's tyranny—returned to take part in an oil-fueled construction boom.

But those days are long gone. When I caught up with Rebar Sadiq, the Kurdistan Regional Government's deputy finance advisor, he painted a grim picture. "The KRG needs more than one billion dollars per month to fit their needs, and we have 40 percent per month of what we had before the war with IS," he told me. "We cannot provide money for investment expenses because our [oil] production is so much less than our expenses. There are a lot of projects that have stopped."

That opening up Iraq's energy resources to the international market would produce oil revenues that would be more than enough to self-finance the country's reconstruction after the 2003 U.S. invasion was a line often trotted out by top American officials. "The oil revenue of that country could bring between 50 and 100 billion dollars over the course of the next two or three years," deputy Defense Secretary Paul Wolfowitz told a congressional panel just days after the war began. "We're dealing with a country that could really finance its own reconstruction, and relatively soon."

It's tough to calculate Iraq's oil revenue generated during the war. The Ministry of Oil and Ministry of Natural Resources in Erbil both publish data, but some of the yearly reports are missing information. Other monitoring sites, such as the U.S. State Department, discontinued their efforts to track oil revenue in Iraq in 2011. And some of that data did not separate the oil revenue between Iraq proper and the Kurdish region. A Brookings report published in July 2013 says Iraq made $495 billion in oil revenue from 2003 to 2013, but Kurdish revenue during the final two years was not included.

International oil companies have paid billions of dollars to Kurdish government officials in the form of capacity building bonuses or infrastructure project payments, but most of those funds did not actually go toward building public infrastructure.

Since the U.S. invasion, the KRG's Ministry of Natural Resources
has signed close to forty agreements with oil corporations. Each
contract varied in the amount of bonuses and infrastructure
costs, but several of them included at least two bonus payments
of $40 million. A U.S. Government Accountability Office report
revealed that anywhere from 100,000 to 300,000 barrels a day
of Iraqi oil were unaccounted for between 2003 and 2007. The
report said the total revenue from the lost oil was between $5
million and $15 million daily, or between $7.3 and $21.6 billion in
total; corruption and smuggling were likely the causes.

Qayyarah is a city dependent on oil production and export,
but the wells have been burning on and off since they were
torched in July 2016; black soot from those fires covers the
houses and businesses that ISIS didn't destroy. Qusai tells
me that few of his friends have returned home since the military
took back Qayyarah, in part because there's not much to return
to. Satellite images show a thick, unbroken cloud of oil smoke
covering a huge swath of the region ever since the fires were set.
Thousands of people who have returned to the surrounding villages are living under it.

When I visited a makeshift medical clinic near Qayyarah,
a doctor tended to a long line of people covered in soot. He told
me he was treating twenty to thirty patients a day for respira-
tory problems or skin infection. Antibiotics and bandages were
in short supply, as were nurses and aides. "When you go and
visit this place, you can feel it in your skin and in your lungs,"
said Amy Christian, a worker for the humanitarian organization Oxfam, who was working on a clean water initiative and

120 also attempting to track medical complaints among residents living near the oil wells. "I myself ended up in the hospital," she told me.

Oxfam's canvassing is among the few efforts being made to get a handle on how smoke and toxins from the well fires are affecting public health. The Iraqi government so far seems missing in action. No one has data on the levels of toxins in the air. The U.N. published a report in November 2016 urging the Iraqi Ministry of Health and Environment to begin collecting data from air monitoring stations and conduct regular health-risk assessments for areas affected by the fires. But no study has been conducted.

According to the UK-based Toxic Remnants of War Network, an environmental group that studies the impact of pollution from conflict, and has been working on the ground in the Qayyarah area, the wells in Qayyarah are filled with heavy sour crude, which contain variable amounts of benzene and n-hexane—toxins that can lead to systemic diseases such as leukemia. Added to this already toxic brew is smoke from burning sulfur. Not only does the Qayyarah heavy crude contain sulfur, but when ISIS blew up the nearby sulfur plant in October 2016, they released an estimated 271 kilotons of sulfur dioxide into the atmosphere over six days. The United Nations Environment Programme reported that the Iraqi government and the World Health Organization were treating over a thousand people experiencing symptoms of suffocation related to sulfur smoke.

Baghdad and Erbil have been feuding over who owns these fields—and thus, who's in charge of extinguishing the fires. The

Iraqi army has special troops trained for putting out well fires, but the army had left the task of fighting ISIS to the Kurdish Peshmerga in the area, who are not even trained to deactivate the booby traps that ISIS had set on the wells.

Many international oil companies have pulled out of the country, rattled by security and corruption issues. In 2017, ExxonMobil pulled out most of its exploration blocks it operated in the Kurdistan region. Chevron pulled out of the Rovi block north of Erbil a year earlier, although the company has continued some exploration activities in the Sarta area. Petroceltic International, an Irish company, and America's Hess Corp. both pulled out of contracts to develop the Dinarta block, citing "significant operational challenges."

However, some companies, such as Genel, Gulf Keystone, and Norway's DNO, are hanging on. Some have even been picking up oil contracts dropped by those who are leaving. Yet, even these firms have had difficulty withstanding the economic costs of remaining in Iraqi Kurdistan, not least because of complications they must face when dealing with the Ministry of Natural Resources, which has at times simply withheld payments that it owes to corporations. In its 2015 annual report, Gulf Keystone warned that nonpayment from the Kurdish government "create[s] a material uncertainty that casts significant doubt upon the group's ability to continue as a going concern." In 2016, the company was on the brink of insolvency, forcing management to undertake a restructuring of the balance sheet. It has rebounded since then.

Some companies have dragged the KRG into arbitration courts to force the government to make payments promised under their contracts. Dana Gas, for example, won a $1.96 billion judgment against the government in a London Court of International Arbitration ruling in November 2015. But that judgment has yet to be paid, pending another hearing on damages. In February 2017, the same court said the Kurdish government owed Dana an additional $121 million for gas that they lifted from the corporation.

Meanwhile, the Kurdish government is still signing contracts with major international trading houses, consultancy groups, and even foreign state-run oil companies, in an effort to greatly increase its oil production. It's not clear yet how much revenue will come of the set of agreements with the Turkish Energy Company over thirteen exploration blocks in Kurdistan, or whether the Kurds' "yes" vote for independence in a referendum that further fueled political tensions with both Baghdad and the government of Turkish President Recep Tayyip Erdogan might derail the deal. Oil prices have recovered somewhat from their lows of $30 a barrel in early 2016, and since then Kurdistan's production has also edged up. The KRG and Russia's Rosneft signed a deal in early 2017 that some analysts say should help ease the international oil companies' anxiety about ensuring that their oil gets to market. The $3 billion deal will run until 2019. The Kurdish government said it was going to use the $1 billion earned up front to pay for government spending, including in the war against ISIS.

And there is another potential bright spot. The Ministry of Natural Resources announced in 2016 that it had hired the global accounting firm Deloitte to carry out an internal audit, with the purpose of examining how much oil revenue has been lost or unaccounted for since 2004. It's a positive sign, but that process has yet to begin. The cycle of ever-dysfunctional politics has generated a feeling among rank-and-file Kurds that something has to change. Ordinary Kurds are hurting and angry.

"Our situation is the way it is not only because of the war, but because the government has no plan in place to save money," says Kasim Asi, a schoolteacher I met in Erbil Governorate. The more I talked to Ahmed Qusai, as the well fires burn around us, the more desperate he grows in Debaga refugee camp. "When the Americans came to Iraq, they told us we would be living in castles, with all the oil investment that would be coming in," he says, redirecting his gaze toward his children washing their feet with a hose in the corner of the container. "They didn't tell us we would be living like this."

Acknowledgments

This book is based on reporting conducted in the Kurdish region of Iraq. I am grateful to all the men and women who invited me into their homes and allowed me to listen to their stories. I could not have written this book without their testimony.

I would also like to thank all the people who, despite the risk, came forward with documents that aided me in my attempt to tell the story of oil corruption in Iraqi Kurdistan.

Thanks also to the media outlets that helped support part of my travels to the region, including *Public Radio International*, *IRIN*, and *International Business Times*. A special thanks to Tom Jennings and the Carey Institute for Global Good for giving me the space I needed to write this book, and to Ken Wells for his advisement on this investigation.

IRAQI KURDISTAN HISTORY

There are dozens of books about the history of Iraqi Kurdistan. The one book I found myself going back to most often was *Kurds, Turks, and Arabs: Politics, Travel and Research in North-Eastern Iraq* by C. J. Edmonds. Published in 1957, Edmunds wrote about his time in Iraq decades earlier, when he was the advisor to the Ministry of the Interior for the government, and he chronicles the political and ethnic stories of the region from 1919–1925. His book is rich with historical information that is hard to find anywhere else, as he provides detailed stories about the many Kurdish tribes in the region and chronicles the saga of their ruling families. *Mesopotamia and Kurdistan in Disguise* by E. B. Soane is also a must read.

OIL IN IRAQ AND KURDISTAN

Most of what has been written about the Kurdish oil sector exists in academic papers and local news reports. The local Kurdish publications, including *Rudaw*, cover the oil sector often in the context of the battle against ISIS. *Iraq Oil Reports*, a trade publication that operates out of Erbil, writes exclusively on the topic, and follows the granular details of the entrance and exit of international oil companies, as well as the production of oil fields in the region.

Greg Muttitt's book *Fuel on the Fire: Oil and Politics in Occupied Iraq* chronicles the gross mismanagement of oil funds and the growing corruption in Baghdad. Muttitt focuses mostly on the oil politics of the southern part of the country, but does get into some of the issues with Kurdish oil contracts.

Steve Coll's *Private Empire: ExxonMobil and American Power*, details the oil giant's courting of Iraq and how it controversially found its way into Kurdistan, over angry objections by the U.S. and Baghdad governments. ExxonMobil operates in dozens of countries around the

128   world, so Iraq was not a big focus. But there is invaluable information
      in the few chapters and sections that deal with the U.S. invasion and its
      aftermath.

IRAQ WAR

My favorite book on the Iraq War is Emma Sky's *The Unraveling: High
Hopes and Missed Opportunities in Iraq.* Sky worked as a British political
advisor (and an advisor to the U.S. military) in Iraq during the 2003
invasion. She was posted in Kirkuk, where she oversaw the political
groups' many skirmishes in the city. As Sky tells the story of the invasion
and how the U.S. dealt with governing issues in Iraq after Saddam, she
also provides unique insights about the everyday realities that service
officers like herself faced, as well as the difficulties she encountered
working within the U.S. coalition.

Seymour Hersh's *Chain of Command: The Road from 9/11 to Abu
Ghraib,* does not focus solely on Iraq, yet it offers some of the most
detailed reporting on the invasion and the following battles. Thomas
Rick's *Fiasco: The American Military Adventure in Iraq* is essential for
someone looking to understand the thinking in the Pentagon prior to the
invasion and the decision making during the war. *Blood on Our Hands:
The American Invasion and Destruction of Iraq* by Nicholas J. S. Davies
chronicles the mistakes made by the United States, and *Saddam Hussein's
Ba'th Party: Inside an Authoritarian Regime* by Joseph Sassoon looks into
the inner workings of the regime in Baghdad.

ISIS

Black Flags: the Rise of ISIS by Joby Warrick is undoubtedly the best book
so far on the history of the extremist group. *ISIS: Inside the Army of Terror
by* Hassan Hassan and Michael Weiss is essential for anyone who wants
to know how ISIS operates. Since it relies on the testimony of Syrians
who work for ISIS, it offers a very unusual view of the group.
Some of the best reporting on the ongoing battle against ISIS is done by
freelancers working for outlets across the world, and by Iraqi journalists

who often help us navigate the confusing terrain of the frontline. Some
of those journalists whose work stands out include Cengiz Yar, Warzer
Jaff, Andrea DiCenzo, Ben Solomon, Arwa Damon, Rukmini Callimachi,
Loveday Morris, and Maya Alleruzzo. Some of the most detailed reports
on abuses that occurred during the battles against ISIS can be found at
Human Rights Watch.

NOTES

INTRODUCTION

12 **one of the worst humanitar-ian disasters:** "War, Politics and Humanitarian Disasters Give Iraq a Perfect Storm of Crises," Traci Tong, *PRI's The World*, August 11, 2014.

13 **pulled out of the region:** "International Oil Companies Pull out of Kurdistan," Dilshad Abdullah, *Al Monitor*, December 2016.

13 **Several oil companies were in debt:** "Gulf Keystone Shares Fall to Record Low Over Debt Revamp," David Sheppard and Neil Hume, *The Financial Times*, April 14, 2016.

13 **civil servants:** "The Curse of Oil in Iraqi Kurdistan," Erin Banco, *PRI*, January 17, 2017.

13 **with plans to develop Iraqi Kurdistan:** "Beneath The Sand," John Cassidy, *The New Yorker*, July 14, 2003.

16 **billions of dollars have disappeared to fraud:** "$7.3 Billion on KRG Fuel Imports Could Have Been Saved with Affordable Gas," Luay Al-Khatteeb, Brookings Institution, June 27, 2015.

16 **classic example of the resource curse:** *Escaping the Resource Curse*, edited by Macartan Humphreys, Jeffrey D. Sachs, and Joseph E. Stiglitz, Columbia University Press, May, 2007.

16 **companies come and go:**   131
All of the companies that have worked in the KRG list their work on their websites. Companies post regular updates about their involvement in KRG ventures and earnings. Further information can be found on regulatory websites such as the Security and Exchange Commission's EDGAR database. Others are listed on similar databases in other countries where the companies list on stock exchanges.

17 **documents released by WikiLeaks:** "Corruption in the Kurdish North," February 19, 2006, Kirkuk, Department of State, WikiLeaks.

18 **145 attacks against journalists:** "Iraqi Kurdistan: Kurdish Journalist Abducted, Killed," Human Rights Watch, August 25, 2016.

19 **ISIS squeezed off oil production:** "ISIS Inc: How Oil Fuels the Jihadi Terrorists," Erika Solomon, Guy Chazan, and Sam Jones, *The Financial Times*, October 14, 2015.

19 **played out in courts in London:** "Dana Gas Venture Seeks $26.5 Billion Damages From Iraq Kurds," Anthony Dipaola, *Bloomberg*, May 30, 2017.

20 **$700 billion in revenues since 2003:** "The Case Against Kurdish Independence," Luay Al-Khatteeb, Middle East Institute, August 15, 2016.

132   20   **80 percent of all of Iraq's funding:** Interview with KRG Ministry of Finance.

20   **20 billion just in the year 2013:** "Corruption in Iraq: Where Did All the Money Go?" Luay Al-Khatteeb, *The National Interest*, May 19, 2016.

20   **Unaoil has been involved in widespread corruption:** "Unaoil's Huge New Corporate Bribery Scandal Explained," Nick Baumann, Akbar Shahid Ahmed, Jessica Schulberg, Paul Blumenthal, *The Huffington Post*, March, 30, 2016.

CHAPTER ONE

24   **The Kurdish military moved in:** "Iraqi Kurds 'Fully Control Kirkuk' as Army Flees," BBC, June 12, 2014.

25   **Kurdish affiliation with Kirkuk:** "Although the Kurdish capital and largest city is Erbil, as Tel Aviv is Israel's functional capital and largest city, the place of Kirkuk in the hearts of the Kurdish population—no matter what their political allegiance—is special," writes Michael J. Kelly in "The Kurdish Regional Constitution within the Framework of the Iraqi Federal Constitution: A Struggle for Sovereignty, Oil, Ethnic Identity, and the Prospects for a Reverse Supremacy Clause," *Penn State Law Review*, Vol. 114, No. 3, 2010, pp. 707–808.

26   **In late 2014, the Kurdish government struck a deal:** "Kurdish Oil Deal with Baghdad Unravels as Tensions Rise," Reuters, March 13, 2015.

29   **Saddam's Arabization policy:** *The Unraveling: High Hopes and Missed Opportunities in Iraq*, Emma Sky, Public Affairs, 2016.

29   **more than 20,000 families who had been forced out:** "Iraq's Disputed Territories: A View of the Political Horizon and Implications For U.S. Policy," Sean Kane, United States Institute of Peace, March 2011.

29   **an excuse to crack down on the opposition:** Ibid.

30   **The story of that struggle/ Iraq's oil history:** "Iraq: The Fight Over Kirkuk's Oil," *Frontline*, August 24, 2006; Bet-Shilmon and Arbella Herutha, 2012; "Iraq's Oil Sector: Past, Present and Future," Amy Myers Jaffe, James A. Baker III, Institute for Public Policy, March, 2007.

31   **the independent Kurdish Republic:** Laizer, 1996; Edmunds, 1957.

32   **Saddam's Anfal genocide:** *Ghosts of Halabja: Saddam Hussein and the Kurdish Genocide*, Michael J. Kelly, Preager, 2008.

32   **Saddam seized control of the oil wealth:** *Into Kurdistan: Frontiers Under Fire*, Sheri Laizer, Zed Books, 1991.

34   **512,000 barrels per day to 430,000:** "Iraq's Southern Oil Exports down by 200,000 bpd," Total Energy Informatics, May 24, 2016.

34   **Signs of this strain aren't hard to find:** "Iraqi Troops Advance in Fallujah to Face Refugee Crisis," Kareem Shaheen, *The Guardian*, June 21, 2016.

36   **Law of the Administration for the State of Iraq for the Transitional Period:** Sky, 2016.

37   **"Do not let the occupation forces appoint people":** Sky, 2016; *Oil and Gas in the Disputed Kurdish Territories: Jurisprudence, Regional Minorities and Natural Resources in a Federal System*, Rex J. Zedalis, Routledge, 2012; "Law of Administration for the State of Iraq for the Transitional Period," Coalition Provisional Authority, March 8, 2004; "The Future of Kirkuk: The Referendum and its Potential Impact on Displacement," Elizabeth Ferris, Brookings Institute—University of Bern Project on Internal Displacement, March 3, 2008.

37   **"For Sale" on Arab homes:** Sky, 2016.

37   **Peter Galbraith:** "U.S. Adviser to Kurds Stands to Reap Oil Profits," James Glanz and Walter Gibbs, *The New York Times*, November 1, 2009. Other materials on Galbraith gathered from interviews with SEC and DOJ sources who investigated Galbraith's connections to oil companies in the KRG; Muttitt, 2012.

38   **British court ordered DNO to pay Galbraith:** based on interviews and documents gathered from SEC, FSA, and DOJ sources who

investigated Galbraith's connection to DNO. Other press reporting includes "Galbraith Admits Financial Stake in Kurdish oil," *Foreign Policy*, October 15, 2009.

39   **Hussain al-Shahristani often threatened to blacklist:** "ExxonMobil's Iraqi Kurdistan Contract Shifts Landscape," April Yee, *The National*, November 14, 2011.

40   **took over oil fields previously run by the North Oil Company:** "Kurdish Forces Seize Oilfields Near Kirkuk," Erika Solomon, *The Financial Times*, July 12, 2014.

CHAPTER TWO

41   **"master of contract negotiations"/Hawrami and oil contracts:** Interview with Delshad Shaban, deputy head of the oil and gas committee in the Kurdish parliament, August, 2016.

44   **technical service agreement:** "Technical Service Contracts," 2B1st Consulting, August 10, 2012.

44   **PSAs are different:** "Production Sharing Agreements: An Economic Analysis," Kirsten Bindemann, Oxford Institute for Energy Studies, October 1999.

45   **greater tax breaks:** I studied the tax breaks offered by the KRG and the bonuses attached to the contracts in a review of original and complete contracts given to me by financial regulatory enforcement officers.

134   46   **The Atrush block:** "Newest Iraqi Gusher Could Make Texas Oilman A Billionaire," Christopher Helman, *Forbes*, September 13, 2012.

47   **company letter to shareholders:** "Bayou Bend Petroleum LTD. Notice of Meeting and Information Circular. In respect of the Annual General and Special Meeting of Shareholders to be held on October 16, 2009," September 14, 2009; interviews with SEC sources; "Certificate of Change of Name," Registrar of Companies, Province of British Columbia Canada, October 21, 2009; "Zebra Holdings & Investments News Release," October 1, 2009.

49   **Oslo Stock Exchange investigated:** Tom Bergin and Steve Slater, "Kurdish Minister Received Market Abuse Emails—Sources," Reuters, April 7, 2012.

50   **Hawrami received emails from Ian Hannam:** "Heritage Oil Chief Executive Defends Ian Hannam Against Market Abuse Accusations," Caroline Binham, *The Financial Times*, July 4, 2013.

50   **Heritage Oil:** "This Man is in Charge of Opening Up One of the Last Oil Frontiers," Andrew Critchlow, *The Telegraph*, December 20, 2014.

50   **Hawrami instructed brokers:** "Minister's Secret £13m Oil Profit," Jon Ungoed-Thomas, *The Sunday Times*, February 21, 2010.

50   **The FSA ended up going after Hannam:** "FSA fines JP Morgan Banker Ian Hannam For Market Abuse," BBC News, April 3, 2012.

CHAPTER THREE

52   **dominated by the Barzani tribe:** Laizer, 1996 and 1991. Other press reporting includes "From Death to Dollars—How Kurds Struck It Rich," Patrick Cockburn, *The Independent*, March 7, 2013; "The Iraqi Kurdish Density after the Kurdish Movement Collapsed in March 1975," Karwan Salih Waisy, *International Journal of Science and Research*, 2013.

53   **A 2006 U.S. State Department cable:** "Corruption in the Kurdish North," February 19, 2006. Kirkuk, Department of State, WikiLeaks.

54   **Diyar Group, Eagle Group:** A compiled list of local contractors was given to me by sources at the SEC and DOJ.

54   **Prime Natural Resources and PetOil:** Approval Judgment In the High Court of Justice, Queens Bench Division, Commercial Court in the case between Western Zagros vs Monde, June 28, 2016. http://ekurd.net/wp-content/uploads/2016/07/Case-No-2013-Folio-308.pdf

55   **Monde Petroleum SA v. Westernzagros Ltd.:** Ibid.

56   **Hawrami imposed terms:** Interview with Delshad Shaban, deputy head of the oil and gas committee in the Kurdish Parliament.

56   **Yassir Al-Fekaiki:** Interviews with two SEC investigators still looking into the case.

58   **the judge ruled:** "Negotiating PSC's—The Dangers of Using Intermediaries," Darrenn Spalding, BRACEWELL, August 20, 2016.

58   **"all it does is cost us":** Emails by Simon Hatfield from SEC and DOJ sources.

CHAPTER FOUR

59   **Rex Wempen:** Wempen's story is detailed in the judgment of "Excalibur Ventures LLC v. Texas Keystone Inc. and Others," The High Court of Justice, Queen's Bench Division, Dec. 13, 2013. https://7kbw.co.uk/wp-content/uploads/2016/05/Excalibur_2.rtf.pdf

60   **Zalmay Khalilzad, then a deputy undersecretary:** "Was the Iraq War Conceived in a Secret 1992 Document?" Zalmay Khalilzad, *The National Interest*, April 18, 2016.

60   **1992 Defense Planning Guidance:** Defense Planning: Guidance 1994–1999, 1992. National Archives.

60   **Dick Cheney told Khalilzad:** Khalilzad, *The National Interest*, 2016; *The Envoy*, Khalilzad, 2016.

60   **Paul Wolfowitz:** Ibid.

61   **"that explains the decision to invade Iraq":** *The Envoy: From Kabul to the White House, My Journey Through a Turbulent World*, Zalmay Khalilzad, St. Martin's Press, 2016.

61   **"The Future of Iraq Project":** 135
Energy Task Force Maps, List of Suitors, National Security Archives, September 22, 2010.

61   **Energy Task Force:** Ibid.

62   **The Iraq Inquiry and Jonny Baxter:** "Witness Transcripts: Mr. Jonny Baxter—Private Hearing," The Iraq Inquiry, June 24, 2010.

63   **Ray Hunt, George W. Bush and KRG oil:** Henry Waxman (D-Calif.), chairman of the Committee on Oversight and Government Reform, congressional write up about Hunt Oil and company entering into Iraq. Document given by SEC and DOJ sources; "Bush Officials Condoned Regional Iraqi Oil Deal," Steven Mufson, *The Washington Post*, July, 3, 2008.

63   **Rex Wempen's biography:** "Excalibur Ventures LLC v. Texas Keystone Inc. and Others."

65   **Wempen meeting Zebari, Yacu, Al-Qabandi:** Ibid.

65   **as far back as the 1950s:** "Iraq's Oil Sector: Past, Present and Future," Amy Meyers Jaffe, James A. Baker III Institute for Public Policy, Rice University, March 2007.

65   **the Chinese and Russians:** National Security Archives, Energy Task Force Maps, List of Suitors, September 22, 2010.

68   **the elite Al-Qassimi family:** "Kurdistan Full of Promising Investment Opportunities," Ibrahim Khalil, *Iraqi News*, May

136   19, 2010. Other information about Al-Qassimi and their oil investment can be found on the Crescent Petroleum website under "operations," on the Abu Dhabi securities and exchange website, and on the TAQA and RAK websites. I traced the major UAE families' oil company board appointments and investments, and sources in the SEC and DOJ told me about the sums of the investments and the political sway UAE investors held over companies invested in the KRG.

68   Texas Keystone, Gulf Keystone, Wempen and Kozel: "Excalibur Ventures LLC v. Texas Keystone Inc. and Others."

69   the Shaikan block: Gulf Keystone-Shaikan contract description, November, 2007.

71   Hawrami warned him: Ibid.

71   judge Elizabeth Gloster: "Excalibur Ventures LLC v. Texas Keystone Inc. and Others."

CHAPTER FIVE

74 $240 billion in annual revenues: Exxon Mobil annual report 2016.

74   Foreign companies like China National Petroleum Corporation: "China Has Head Start over West for Iraq Oil," Simon Webb, Reuters, August 28, 2008. "Threats and Responses: Energy Industry; Iraq Cancels Oil Contract With 3 Russian Companies," Steven Lee Myers, *The New York Times*, December 13, 2002.

75   the West Qurna-1 field: "ExxonMobil wins $50 Bn Contract to Develop West Qurna Oilfield," Martin Chulov, *The Guardian*, November 5, 2009.

76   Ali Khedery: "Special Report: How Exxon Helped Make Iraqi Kurdistan," Dmitry Zhdannikov, Isabel Coles, and Ned Parker, Reuters, December 3, 2014.

77   meetings in Erbil, London, and Dubai: Interviews with SEC and DOJ sources.

77   Soon after, ExxonMobil signed: Zhdannikov, Coles, and Parker, 2014.

77   Exxon executives informed the State Department: "Exxon Signs Kurd Deals, Baghdad Warns," Tom Bergin and Ahmed Rasheed, Reuters, November 11, 2013. "How a Rex Tillerson Oil Deal Nearly Sparked an Iraqi-Kurdish War," Stephen Snyder, *PRI's The World*, January 5, 2017.

77   lie in territory that continues to be disputed: "How Exxon, Under Rex Tillerson, Won Iraqi Oil Fields and Nearly Lost Iraq," Missy Ryan and Steven Mufson, *The Washington Post*, January 9, 2017; "Exxon, Kurdistan Visit Disputed Iraqi Oil Block," Ahmed Rasheed, Reuters, February 1, 2013.

77   none other than Jeffrey: "Exxon Hires ex-U.S. Officials to Navigate Iraq," Ben Lando, Iraq Oil Report, February 8, 2013. SEC and DOJ sources interviewed for this book said James Jeffrey was an unofficial advisor working on the Exxon negotiation with the Ministry of Natural Resources. Jeffrey says he was not working in an official capacity during the negotiations, but admits he did play a part in smoothing tensions when the company signed with the KRG and angered Baghdad.

78 **RiceHadleyGates:** Lando, 2013.

79 **pipelines from Kurdistan to Turkey:** "Exclusive: Turkey, Iraqi Kurdistan Clinch Major Energy Pipeline Deals," Humeyra Pamuk and Orhan Coskun, Reuters, November 6, 2013; "Hacked Emails Reveal Details Of Exxon's Kurdistan Activity," Ben Van Heuvelen, Iraqi Oil Report, December 20, 2016.

80 **Turkey received 5 percent:** "Turkey's KRG energy partnership," Gonul Tol, *Foreign Policy*, January 29, 2013; "Turkish Ambivalence Toward Kurdish Energy: Between Economics and Politics," Dr. Volkan Ozdemir, Institute for Energy Markets and Policies, November 2014.

80 **Halkbank:** "KRG Statement on First Oil Sales Through Pipeline Export," Ministry of Natural Resources, May 23, 2014.

80 **al-Maliki even asked President Obama:** "UPDATE 1-Iraq PM Asks Obama to Stop Exxon-Kurdistan Oil Deal," Ahmed Rasheed, Reuters, June 19, 2012.

80 **ExxonMobil eventually relinquished its interests:** "Exxon Pulls Out of Three Exploration Blocks in Kurdistan: Iraq Oil Report," Reuters, December 6, 2016.

80 **"Some companies didn't meet contractual deadlines":** "Exxon Cuts Kurdistan Portfolio by Half," Ben Lando, Patrick Osgood, Ben Van Heuvelen, *Iraq Oil Report*, December 6, 2016.   137

80 **Turkey to deploy five hundred troops:** "Islamic State Clash with Turkish Troops at Iraqi Base: Military Sources," Reuters, March 22, 2016; "Turkish Boots on the Ground," IRIS Iraq Report, The American University of Iraq Sulaimani, Institute of Regional and International Studies.

81 **Iraqi court issued an arrest warrant:** "Iraqi Officials Say to Arrest Former Governor if he Reenters Mosul," Rudaw, January 28, 2017.

81 **the man whose blessing ExxonMobil needed:** "The Enemy You Know and the Ally You Don't," Benjamin Bahney, Patrick B. Johnson, Patrick Ryan, *Foreign Policy*, June 23, 2015.

81 **"We must be part of this contract":** "ExxonMobil's Deal with Iraqi Kurdistan Fuels Uproar," Adel Shaymaa, *Al Monitor*, June 20, 2012.

CHAPTER SIX

82 **Peter Galbraith:** "Galbraith, Envoy Who Advised Kurds, Gets Millions in Oil Deal," James Glanz, *The New York Times*, October 6, 2010.

83 **Pinemont and Norsk Hydro:** "Report to Norsk Hydro ASA

138   Board of Directors," Shearman & Sterling LLP, October 6, 2008; "Recent Investments," Pinemont, http://www.pinemont.com/recent-investments/

83 "Norwegian businessman" and a "foreign politician": "Report to Norsk Hydro ASA Board of Directors."

83 Endre Rosjo: Companies House, a UK database that registers company information and makes it available to the public. https://beta.companieshouse.gov.uk/officers/SQTRRKvMI3uFC9RSMa_nziZNyzE/appointments

84 A British court awarded them between $55 and $75 million: Glanz, and confirmed by financial regulatory enforcement officers in the U.S. and UK who investigated the case.

84 "The business interest, including my investment into Kurdistan, was consistent with my political views": "Former Diplomat Denies Oil Dealings Influenced Views," Farah Stockman, *Boston Globe,* October 15, 2009.

85 General Jay Garner: "Vast Appoints General Jay Garner to the Board of Directors and Colonel Richard Nabb as Vice President-Kurdistan Operations and Announces Stock Options," Vast Exploration, June 19, 2008.

85 Hunt Oil's dealings: Henry Waxman (D-Calif.), chairman of the Committee on Oversight and Government Reform, congressional write up about Hunt Oil and company entering into Iraq, document given by SEC and DOJ sources; "Bush Officials Condoned Regional Iraqi Oil Deal," Steven Mufson, *The Washington Post,* July, 3, 2008.

87 Nadhim Zahawi: "British Politician Earns Massive Salary From Oil Company as Local Iraqis Suffer Downfall," *International Business Times,* April 30, 2016; Parliamentary registry documents in the United Kingdom.

87 earned more than $350,000 a year: UK parliamentary registry: https://publications.parliament.uk/pa/cm/cmregmem/170306/zahawi_nadhim.htm

CHAPTER SEVEN

89 The five containers held brand new sport utility vehicles: Maersk shipping documents and emails from SEC investigators that detail how Crescent sent the SUVs to Iraq.

91 "bonus" payments: Often the various types of bonuses are not included on contracts publicly listed online, but in appendices. Examples of those bonuses were shown to me by SEC sources. The investigators who tracked FCPA violations also compiled capacity building bonus lists.